ELECTIONS AND VOTING
BEHAVIOUR IN BRITAIN

CONTEMPORARY POLITICAL STUDIES SERIES

Series Editor: John Benyon, *Director, Centre for the Study of Public Order, University of Leicester*

A series which provides authoritative yet concise introductory accounts of key topics in contemporary political studies.

ELECTIONS AND VOTING BEHAVIOUR IN BRITAIN

Second Edition

DAVID DENVER

HARVESTER
WHEATSHEAF

New York   London   Toronto   Sydney   Tokyo   Singapore

First published 1994 by
Harvester Wheatsheaf
Campus 400, Maylands Avenue
Hemel Hempstead
Hertfordshire, HP2 7EZ
A division of
Simon & Schuster International Group

Typeset in 10/12pt Times
by Dorwyn Ltd, Rowlands Castle, Hants.
Printed and bound in Great Britain by
Biddles Ltd, Guildford and King's Lynn

British Library Cataloguing in Publication Data

A catalogue record for this book is available from
the British Library

ISBN 0 7450 1602 2

2 3 4 5 95

CONTENTS

PREFACE TO THE FIRST EDITION

Elections in Britain, as in all liberal democracies, are central to the political process. They involve, to some extent, almost the entire adult population and inform almost every aspect of political life. Not surprisingly, interest in elections is also widespread – from students and teachers of British politics at school or undergraduate level to journalists, members of political parties and many otherwise 'ordinary' people. The problem for people like these is that in recent years the specialised literature dealing with elections and voting behaviour in Britain has grown enormously and has become highly technical and statistically complex.

My intention in this book is to introduce readers to this wider literature in a way that is as non-technical as I can make it. I hope that there is enough 'meat' in the book to satisfy undergraduates and A-level students but I hope, too, that those whose interest in the subject is more general will find the book rewarding. With this audience in mind, I have had to simplify some rather complicated material and I apologise in advance to any of the authors discussed who may think that I have over-simplified their arguments, theories or conclusions. *Really* serious students of electoral analysis must consult the primary literature themselves.

Talking about, reading about, observing, participating in and even doing research on elections are not just for 'serious students', however. If any readers who are not currently students acquire from this book a fuller understanding of trends in British elections and a keener, more critical interest in the electoral process then it will have served one of its major purposes.

Preparing the book has, of course, involved me in numerous debts. I am grateful to the following for permission to reproduce material: American Enterprise Institute, Butterworth Scientific Ltd, Cambridge University Press, David Butler, Ivor Crewe, Colin Crouch, Patrick Dunleavy, Anthony Heath and William Miller.

Jeremy Mitchell commented helpfully on an early draft of the manuscript and John Bochel also gave me the benefit of his sage advice. Russell Price, with his enviable eye for detail, made numerous useful suggestions on points of style. I am especially grateful to my colleague Gordon Hands who read and re-read numerous drafts and with whom I have had lengthy and profitable discussions at every stage of writing. The general editor of the series, John Benyon, and Philip Cross of Philip Allan Ltd were valued sources of encouragement and advice. Finally, my wife Barbara not only supported and encouraged me and tolerated a good deal, but also mastered a new word processing system to prepare the manuscript.

Despite the best efforts of all of these, there remain, no doubt, errors of interpretation and (just possibly) fact. Responsibility for these is mine.

David Denver
Lancaster, 1989

PREFACE TO THE SECOND EDITION

The comments that I have received from colleagues about the first edition of the book have been generally encouraging. In this edition, therefore, the structure of the book is broadly the same, although I have taken the opportunity not only to update data and incorporate the most recent literature but also to include some new topics (e.g. volatility) and clarify my ideas on others.

I have received conflicting advice about the introductory statistical material in the first chapter but have decided to retain it as I think that some grasp of the basic ideas presented there is essential for understanding the rest of the book.

Almost anyone writing about British elections owes a debt of gratitude to the British Election Study team. The data from their surveys of the 1992 election have been made available with remarkable rapidity and the fact that I have been able to use these data has made this edition much more valuable than would have been possible otherwise.

Finally, I should like to thank Clare Grist of Simon & Schuster and June Rye for help of various kinds in the preparation of this edition.

David Denver
Lancaster, November 1993

THE STUDY OF ELECTIONS AND ELECTORAL BEHAVIOUR

Why study elections?

Elections are fun. In the first half of the nineteenth century, part of the fun involved the voters getting roaring drunk at the candidates' expense, brawling in the street with opponents and pelting them with rotten fruit. The practice of candidates 'treating' voters was effectively ended by the Second Reform Act of 1867 which greatly enlarged the electorate. There were now simply too many voters to treat. In addition, in 1872 the Ballot Act made voting secret (previously voters had had to declare their choice in public) so that candidates could no longer check that the voters they had treated actually voted for them. Finally, in 1883, the Corrupt Practices Act outlawed treating (much to the disappointment of most voters, one suspects).

Despite this, elections continued to be a form of public entertainment until well into the twentieth century. In 1922 a crowd of 10,000 assembled to hear the declaration of the general election result in Dundee and were rewarded with the news that the sitting member, Winston Churchill, had been defeated by a Prohibitionist!

Today, elections continue to be enjoyed by all sorts of people. Candidates and party workers often experience a sense of exhilaration during campaigns; people in the media are caught up in the excitement of reporting a major national event; television presenters get to use all sorts of computer gadgetry; pollsters, analysts and pundits find themselves in great demand. Even the mass of ordinary voters who now largely 'spectate' on election campaigns appear to enjoy the race, some of them betting on the outcome and many watching campaign reports and party broadcasts on television. Election night parties are not uncommon.

Studying elections is also fun. Some people collect stamps, some are train spotters, others pore over cricket statistics in *Wisden*. But there are also 'election buffs' around the country who collect, collate and analyse election results. Part of the fascination is the sheer mass of information available. In British general elections there are results for 651 constituencies to be looked at,[1] but in addition there are elections to the European Parliament and elections for local councils, which involve many thousands of wards and electoral divisions. Local election results in Britain are not centrally collected and published by the state, so even acquiring a comprehensive collection of results is a major exercise in detective work.[2]

Election results are also fascinating because they are numerical in form and numbers can be analysed endlessly. Voting figures can be aggregated, averaged, graphed and used to construct maps. Some academic studies of electoral behaviour take statistical manipulation so far that they become incomprehensible to all but about a hundred people in the whole country! But a great deal can be done with just a few elementary techniques.

The fact that elections yield masses of quantitative data amenable to statistical analysis, together with the rapid development of computers, partly explains the huge growth in the academic literature on elections over the past thirty years or so. But there is more to it than that. Elections are studied because they are important. Most people would agree that it is the existence of free, competitive elections that distinguishes political systems that we normally call 'democratic' from others. Different versions of democratic theory attach different weights to elections and assign them different functions, but all see elections as central to democracy.

In traditional democratic theory, elections give sovereignty or ultimate power to the citizens. It is through elections that the citizen participates in the political process and ultimately determines the personnel and policies of governments. Only a government that is elected by the people is a legitimate government. Other democratic theorists view elections as only one among a number of channels of citizen influence, stressing the indirect nature of influence through the electoral process, and an influential version of democratic theory suggests that elections simply allow citizens a choice between competing élites. The existence of free elections remains, none the less, the essential difference between democratic and non-democratic states. Even theories such as Marxism, that wish to deny that elections permit the people to have any real influence over the state, nevertheless agree that elections are important means of binding people to the political system by creating, in the Marxists' view, an illusion of influence.

Exactly how and how much elections affect what governments do is, then, a matter of some debate. At a minimum, however, it is clear that they provide a peaceful way of changing governments (and this is not unimportant given the number of governments around the world that are removed by violence). Elections are also the means by which the great mass of citizens can participate directly in the political process, and in Britain millions of citizens do participate in this way. For most, voting is the only overtly political action that is regularly undertaken. Finally, elections also make governments accountable to the electorate, at least once every five years in Britain. Voters can pass judgement on the government and either keep it in office or replace it.

Undeniably, general elections are major national events that precipitate greatly increased political activity, discussion, interest and media coverage. On election night, crowds gather in Trafalgar Square and the attention of almost the whole nation is at least partly engaged by the election. Next day, the front pages of all newspapers are entirely devoted to election news.

These would be reasons enough for studying elections. But it is also clear that elections do make a difference to what happens. Although there might be some debate about the precise extent or importance of the difference made when one party rather than another wins an election, and it is certainly true that governments of any party are constrained by external events over which they have little control, it seems to strain credulity to suggest, for example, that the Conservative victory in the 1979 general election has had little effect on subsequent events.

Elections, then, are central to democracy, occasion mass political behaviour and determine who governs, and thus affect the lives of all of us. By studying them we seek to deepen our understanding of how a key process of democracy operates, to discover how citizens make their voting decisions and to explain election outcomes.

In this book I discuss some of the major themes that have emerged from studies of British elections and electoral behaviour. The literature on this topic is vast, detailed and sometimes technically complex. It is necessary, therefore, to paint with rather broad brush strokes. I hope, however, that readers will gain an enhanced understanding of recent developments in this important area of national political life, and perhaps also acquire the enthusiasm to pursue the subject in more detail elsewhere.

As a preliminary, however, since even a basic understanding of election results or of the electoral studies literature inevitably involves dealing with numerical data, the remainder of this chapter is devoted to an explanation of some of the statistical techniques that are commonly used in electoral analysis.

Analysing election results

Elections yield masses of quantitative data. The election results themselves and the results of opinion polls and other surveys form the bases of most books or articles about elections and voting behaviour. As a result, such studies almost invariably contain some statistical analysis. In order to appreciate this literature fully or to undertake analysis on one's own, it is important to have a basic grasp of the nature of different kinds of data and of some elementary statistical techniques.

Types of data

Figure 1.1 differentiates four types of data according to *level* and *scale* of measurement.[3]

First, what does level of data mean? *Aggregate*-level data refer to an aggregate or collectivity. We know, for example, that in the Lancaster constituency in the 1992 general election there was a

Level Scale	Aggregate	Individual
Interval	a	c
Nominal	b	d

Figure 1.1   Types of data.

78.8 per cent turn-out and the distribution of votes was 45.6 per cent Conservative, 39.2 per cent Labour and 14.1 per cent Liberal Democrat (with the remainder being won by 'others'). This result was obtained by totting up, or aggregating, the number of people who voted and the party for which they voted. From the final result we do not know whether or how any individual voted but we do know something about the collectivity of voters in the constituency. It is an important feature of aggregate data that they cannot be used to infer anything about the behaviour or characteristics of individuals. Other examples of aggregate data are the percentage of council tenants in a ward, the number of unemployed people in a constituency, the percentage of manual workers in the north of England, and the change in Labour's share of the vote between 1987 and 1992 over the country as a whole.

If, however, I had organised a sample survey in the Lancaster constituency, I would have sent out interviewers to ask questions of individual voters. By asking the right questions we could find exactly what the individuals in the sample did in the election. This would yield *individual*-level data.

Turning now to scale of measurement, *interval*-scale data refer to numerical information that can be plotted on a scale that has a number of fixed points, each an equal distance apart. A person's height, for example, is measured in a precise number of feet and inches (or metres and centimetres). More relevant from our point of view is the fact that anything that can be expressed as a percentage is on an interval scale from 0 to 100. *Nominal*-scale data, on the other hand, refer to information that can only be assigned to one of a number of categories. The categories are discrete and do not imply any ascending or descending scale. Thus, 'party voted for' is nominal. A person votes Conservative, Labour, Liberal Democrat or something else, and these are categories rather than points on a scale. The same is true of sex, religion, occupation, ethnic group, type of housing, opinion on nuclear weapons and so on.

Matters like these about which we have information — whether related to individuals or constituencies — are known as 'variables'. These are simply things that vary. Thus sex, religion and opinions vary from person to person. Similarly, turn-out and party shares of the vote vary from constituency to constituency and from one election to another. Generally in electoral analysis some variables are thought of as *dependent*, that is their variation is caused or influenced by something else. The dependent variable — an individual's vote or the share of the vote obtained by a party, for example — is what is to be explained. *Independent* variables are factors that do the explaining. Thus if we take the variables sex and vote, it is possible that sex might explain vote — vote is dependent — but it is hard to conceive of a person's vote influencing his or her sex!

Characteristically, individual data are of the nominal type and aggregate data are interval-scale. In other words, the cells indicated 'a' and 'd' in Figure 1.1 are the commonest forms of data. But data that would fit into cells 'b' and 'c' are also found. Thus, constituencies could be categorised according to the party that holds them ('b') or individuals could be given a score out of ten on a series of questions testing political knowledge ('c').

None the less, for the sake of clarity my discussion of interval-scale data analysis will be confined to aggregate data and, in the next section, I will treat nominal data as survey-derived data.

Sample surveys and the analysis of nominal data

Individual-level data, on which many studies of voting behaviour are based, are normally collected by means of sample surveys. I do not propose to discuss here the statistical basis of sampling or the various kinds of samples.[4] It is enough for students of voting behaviour to know that, given an appropriate sample, electoral analysts can make statements about the population from which the sample was taken with a certain margin of error and 'level of confidence'. The reliability and accuracy of survey results varies with the type and size of sample used. As a rule of thumb, however, in reputable studies it is usually highly probable (95 per cent certain) that a sample figure will be within two or three points either side of the true figure for the population as a whole. For example, if an appropriate survey found that 50 per cent of major-party voters among *Sun* readers voted Conservative in the 1992 election (which is, in fact, what was found by the British Election Study survey), then it can be demonstrated mathematically that it is 95 per cent certain that among all *Sun* readers the proportion was 50 per cent plus or minus about three points (i.e. between 47 per cent and 53 per cent).

The important point to note is that figures derived from surveys should not be regarded as precisely accurate. They are *estimates* of the true situation among the population being studied. Put another way, surveys are liable to sampling error, a fact that authors sometimes forget when they get carried away with the apparent precision of the figures produced from their surveys.

Surveys are also liable to other sources of error. Questions may be ambiguous or unclear, may lead respondents to give particular answers, or may be interpreted by the respondents in a way that was not intended by the questionnaire designer. Mistakes may be made by interviewers in recording answers; slips happen during the tedious operations of converting answers to numbers and transferring them to a computer. Even so, sample surveys are generally reliable and powerful research tools. They have become an indispensable part of electoral analysis and have played a crucial role in advancing our understanding of electoral behaviour.

Academic survey studies of voting behaviour were pioneered in the 1940s in the United States. The first survey of voting behaviour in Britain was a local study carried out in the constituency of Greenwich in 1950 (Benney, Gray and Pear, 1956). Further local surveys followed in the 1950s but it was not until 1963 that the first national survey study was undertaken under the direction of David Butler and Donald Stokes (Butler and Stokes, 1969). Although 1963 was not an election year, this was the first of a series of national surveys carried out at every general election since 1964 under the auspices of the British Election Study (BES). The results of all these surveys are held on computer at the social science data archive at Essex University and researchers in the field can get copies of the data files. These are a real treasure trove and have formed the basis of numerous books and scholarly articles dealing with voting in Britain.

National surveys are expensive, however. There have been and continue to be many more limited surveys. Researchers have surveyed voters in particular localities and specific groups of voters such as women, 'affluent workers', young people and members of ethnic minority groups.

A public opinion poll is a type of survey, as are the 'exit' polls regularly conducted for both television channels at by-elections and general elections.[5] Like academic surveys, these polls produce a great deal of individual data. Most people pay attention to political polls only at election time, when they achieve high visibility by giving almost daily figures for the voting intentions of the electorate. They have, indeed, become an important and controversial feature of modern election campaigns (see Chapter 5). In fact, however, polls monitor the opinions of the electorate continuously. The Gallup organisation, for example, produces a regular monthly report which, in addition to current voting intention figures, records details of the voters' perceptions of party leaders, government performance, current issues and much else.[6]

Polling firms are, of course, commercial organisations. They are not particularly interested in obtaining the kind of detailed information about voting choice and the factors affecting it that academics study. Poll interviews tend, therefore, to be much shorter than interviews for major academic surveys — often being conducted in the street — and the information sought from voters is normally confined to a few obvious attributes such as age, sex, housing tenure and occupation. None the less, polls constitute a valuable source of individual data. They provide regular monthly data and their results are analysed and published very rapidly. Just two days after the 1992 general election, commentators were using opinion poll results to discuss voting patterns in the election.[7] In contrast, it takes months, if not years, for reports on major academic surveys to become available.

As noted above, surveys can be used to obtain both nominal- and interval-scale data about individuals. Typically, however, nominal-scale data are more commonly derived from surveys. Normally, the first step in analysing data of this kind is to ascertain *frequency distributions*. This simply means determining how many survey

Table I.I   Vote in 1992 (%).

Did not vote	Con.	Lab.	Lib. Dem.	Others	Refused to say
13	39	29	15	3	2 (N = 2,843)

Source: BES 1992 cross-section survey.

respondents fall into each of the nominal categories being used. For convenience, the numbers are usually converted into percentages. An example is given in Table 1.1 which shows (almost) the full range of answers given when respondents to the 1992 BES survey were asked how they had voted in the general election.

It will be noticed, first, that the percentages have been rounded to whole numbers. Since surveys involve only samples of the population, results based on them are estimates of the true figure for the population and there is therefore little point in giving the results to two decimal places! Second, the number of cases upon which the percentages are based is shown in the table (N=2,843). This is good practice since percentages based on small numbers (or 'N's) are inherently unreliable.[8] The sample size in this case is very large — polling firms usually use a national sample of about 1,200 people in order to generalise about the British electorate.

Single-variable analysis of this kind does not take us very far. Usually we want to investigate the relationship between two or more variables. In this case, for example, we might want to test the hypothesis that party choice (the dependent variable) is affected by whether people have manual or non-manual occupations (the independent variable). This is certainly not an original hypothesis but it will serve to illustrate how relationships of this kind are investigated. This is done by constructing *cross-tabulations* or *contingency tables*.

The idea behind cross-tabulation is not difficult to grasp. We have six categories of response to a question on voting and all respondents are assigned to a category. We now divide respondents additionally into one of the ten categories into which their occupations were originally coded (never had a job, professional, employers and managers, intermediate non-manual, junior non-manual, skilled manual, semi-skilled manual, unskilled manual, other and unclassifiable). There are now sixty potential categories (6 × 10) into which individuals may be allocated, and each respondent is put into one of them by, as it were, looking first at how they voted and then at their occupational status. If this were done by hand it would take a long time. It is not so long, in fact, since cross-tabulations were created using punched cards and a machine called a card-sorter or even, strange as it may seem, knitting needles! But now computers produce tables in seconds.

When presented in the form of a table, the categories constitute the *cells* of the table. A table of sixty cells would be very large and difficult to read, however, so it is important to try to simplify the data for presentation. It seems sensible in this case, for example, to start by excluding respondents who did not vote, voted 'other' or refused to say how they voted, since we are not (for the purposes of this analysis) interested in these respondents. The number of cells is now reduced to thirty. When we consider the independent variable, occupation, respondents who had never had a job, or who for some other reason could not be assigned to the manual or the non-manual category, can be left out. Finally, the remainder can be combined into two categories of occupation — non-manual and manual. This leaves us with a table of just six cells. It is standard practice to combine categories and to present only selected cells of tables in this way. There will always be categories for respondents who have failed to answer a question or given an unintelligible answer, which can be omitted; otherwise, the selection depends upon the particular question being investigated.

The reduced cross-tabulation of party choice by occupational class is shown in Table 1.2. The exclusion of some cells has reduced the original number of respondents from 2,843 to 2,272. The table shows that there is a clear relationship between type of occupation and vote in 1992, much as we would expect. Non-manual (white-collar) workers are more likely to vote Conservative and less likely to vote Labour than are manual workers. There is less difference

Table 1.2 Party choice by occupational class, 1992 (%).

	Non-manual	*Manual*
Conservative	56	36
Labour	24	51
Liberal Democrat	21	14
	(N = 1,279)	(N = 993)

Source: BES 1992 cross-section survey.

Table 1.3 Occupational class by party choice, 1992 (%).

	Conservative	Labour	Liberal Democrat
Non-manual	67	37	67
Manual	33	63	33
	(N = 1,063)	(N = 808)	(N = 401)

Source: BES 1992 cross-section survey.

between the two groups in respect of propensity to vote for the Liberal Democrats.

The percentages shown in the table are, as I have explained, estimates from a sample of the electorate. We need to know, therefore, whether the differences found in the sample are likely to reflect real differences among the population at large. To discover this, tests of statistical significance are normally applied. These are rather complicated (see Startup and Whittaker, 1982, ch. 9) but frequently authors simply report that what they have found is 'significant at the 95 per cent level' or 'p < .05'. This means that there is only a 5 per cent chance, or a probability of less than .05, that the difference found in the sample does not reflect a difference in the population as a whole. In other words, the difference found is statistically significant; it is not due to chance.

The information contained in Table 1.2 could have been presented in another way. Instead of using the number of people in each occupational group as the basis for calculating the percentages, I could have used the number of people who voted for each party. Table 1.3 shows how the data look if this is done.

It must be emphasised that the numbers that were originally in the cells of Table 1.3 are exactly the same as those used to construct Table 1.2. It is simply that the percentages have been calculated on different bases. The two tables tell us different things. Table 1.2 tells us how people with different occupations voted. Table 1.3 tells us the occupational make-up of each party's voters. Thus, 51 per cent of manual workers voted Labour and manual workers constituted 63 per cent of Labour voters. Any two-variable cross-tabulation can be analysed and interpreted in two different ways like this.

Table 1.2 showed that there was a relationship between occupation and vote. We might want to ask, however, whether this

Table 1.4   Party choice by occupational class and self-assessed class, 1992 (%).

	Self-assessed 'middle'		Self-assessed 'working'		Self-assessed 'none'	
	Non-manual	Manual	Non-manual	Manual	Non-manual	Manual
Conservative	61	50	32	20	62	45
Labour	15	34	49	70	18	39
Liberal Democrat	24	16	18	10	20	16
(N)	(285)	(100)	(256)	(384)	(714)	(492)

Source: BES 1992 cross-section survey.

relationship continues to hold when other factors are taken into account or 'controlled'. For example, we might consider whether the manual/non-manual difference still exists if we take account of the class to which people *think* they belong. We do this by constructing a three-way table. The logic of this is not difficult to understand. Having created the original two-way table with 60 cells, each cell is then divided into 6 (this is the number of categories into which answers to a question on self-assessed class were classified). We now have a table of no less than 360 cells into one of which each individual respondent can be placed. A table of this size would be very unwieldy, to say the least, and so, as before, cells can be omitted and combined. By doing this I have reduced the data to a table of just 18 cells (see Table 1.4).

The table displays some complicated relationships but the basic point of Table 1.3 — that non-manual workers are more inclined to vote Conservative and less likely to vote Labour than manual workers — is confirmed even when self-assessed class is taken into account.

More generally, the table illustrates two important problems with cross-tabulation analysis. First, as more variables are brought into the analysis the number of cells in tables multiplies rapidly. With just three variables in the analysis we already have a basic table of 360 cells. If we were to add another variable — age, for instance — the resulting table would be truly enormous. Tables quickly become difficult to present clearly and to understand. More importantly, the number of cases within cells on which percentages are based rapidly diminishes. We started in Table 1.1 with

2,843 respondents; by Table 1.4 we are down to 2,231 and the column totals range from 100 to 714. The addition of further variables would further reduce these.[9]

The second problem revealed by our example is that of multiple effects. While Table 1.4 shows that there are consistent differences between manual and non-manual workers, it is also the case that how people assess their class affects party choice. Manual workers who see themselves as middle class are more likely to vote Conservative than those who see themselves as working class, and so on. If we were to add a fourth variable we might find that it too had an independent effect.

The problem is how to measure and assess these different effects. There is a statistical technique for doing this, called log-linear analysis. Using this technique, the numbers actually in the cells of a table are compared with the numbers that would be there under various hypotheses (or models) about the relationships between the variables involved. When the model that best fits the actual data is identified, the significance of each of the independent variables and of interactions between them can be estimated. This is an advanced technique that can only be performed using a computer and it has not as yet been widely used in the literature on voting behaviour (see, however, Heath, Jowell and Curtice, 1985; Heath et al., 1991).

Another, more common, way of coping with this difficulty is to treat nominal variables as if they were of the interval kind by assigning numeric values to the categories. This allows powerful statistical techniques which can be used with interval-scale data, in particular multiple regression analysis (see p. 17), to be applied to data that are essentially nominal.

Assigning numeric values is quite easy in the case of dichotomous variables. Sex, for example, could be scored 1 = female, 0 = male. When there are more than two categories, things get a little more complicated. In these cases we have to create a series of dichotomous variables, one for each category, and score them as above. Thus, to convert 'party voted for' into interval form requires a variable scored 1 = voted Conservative, 0 = did not vote Conservative; then a second variable scored 1 = voted Labour, 0 = did not vote Labour; and then third or fourth variables for other parties scored in the same way. The artificiality of this process is illustrated by the fact that variables created in this way are known as 'dummy' variables.

The analysis of interval-scale data

Election results essentially consist of a series of interval-scale variables. In a general election, for instance, we can easily calculate the percentage turn-out and the percentage share of the vote for each party in every constituency, which constitute the most obvious dependent variables in electoral analysis.

The usual starting point for analysing data of this kind is to describe the *central tendency* (or average) and *dispersion* (or spread) of a set of scores. We might want to know the average constituency turn-out in the 1992 election, for example, and the extent of variation in turn-out from one constituency to another. The measures most commonly employed to do this are the mean and the standard deviation and these are explained in any introductory statistics textbook (see, for example, Startup and Whittaker, 1982, chs. 2 and 3).

As with nominal data, however, analysis of a single variable does not take us very far. Normally we would want to relate one or more dependent variables to other factors that might be presumed to influence them. This is frequently done using *correlation* and *regression* analysis. This is not as awesome as it sounds. It is not necessary for a student of voting behaviour to know how to calculate the statistics involved. Indeed, most political scientists would not know how to begin to calculate a correlation coefficient or a regression equation. Even if they did, the calculations would take hours to complete if there were a reasonable number of cases involved. Nowadays, the calculations are all done by computer, and all that the student needs to know is what the results mean and the basic principles involved.

An understanding of these basic principles can be gained by starting with a piece of graph paper and a small set of data. For illustrative purposes, I will use per cent working class and per cent Labour share of the vote in fifteen English constituencies in the 1987 general election.[10] The line along the bottom of the graph paper is called the x-axis and is used to measure the independent variable (per cent working class). The vertical line on the left is called the y-axis and is used to measure the dependent variable (per cent Labour). Each of the fifteen constituencies can be located on the graph by checking its score on each of the two variables and plotting its position. This creates a

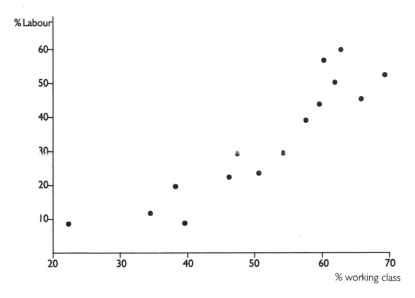

Figure 1.2   Scatter diagram of % working class by % Labour.

'scatter diagram' and Figure 1.2 shows the diagram for my fifteen constituencies.

Simply by looking at the diagram we can see that there is a relationship between the two variables. As the percentage of working-class people in a constituency increases, the share of the vote obtained by Labour also tends to increase. But we can be more precise than this. Looking at the pattern in the diagram, we can imagine drawing a straight line that 'best fits' the points. In fact there exists a unique straight line that does 'best fit' the data, in the sense that the sum of the distances between each point and the line is at the minimum possible.[11] The problem is to find out what this line is.

Any straight line on a graph can be described by an equation of the form $y = a + b(x)$, where y is the dependent variable score, x is the independent variable score and a and b are two numbers which we do not yet know.[12] This is a regression equation. For any particular set of data the values of a and b can be calculated (very quickly by a computer) to give the equation for the best fitting line. For the data in Figure 1.2 the equation is

$$\text{\% Labour} = -30.4 + 1.20 \,(\text{\% working class})$$

To draw the line, we simply solve the equation for two convenient scores on per cent working class. Thus, when per cent working class = 40, per cent Labour = 17.6 and when per cent working class = 70, per cent Labour = 53.6. If these are plotted and joined up, we have the best fitting line.

The regression equation tells us exactly how the two variables are related. We can 'predict' the per cent Labour when we know the per cent working class just by solving the equation. 'Prediction' in this context has nothing to do with foretelling the future. It is simply that when we know a constituency's score on the independent variable we can calculate what its score on the dependent variable 'ought' to be, given the overall relationship discovered. We could, therefore, identify deviant cases, where the Labour vote is noticeably higher or lower than it 'ought' to be.

Knowing how two variables are related is important but it is only half of the story. We also need to know how strongly they are related. The same regression line could be the best fit of a series of points that were well spread out around the line or of another series closely clustered around it. In the latter case the relationship would be a stronger one. The strength of a relationship is measured by a statistic called the *correlation coefficient* (properly the Pearson product-moment correlation coefficient), which is signified as r. The value of r varies from +1 through 0 to –1. Where it is positive, this indicates (unsurprisingly) that the two variables are positively related. This means that as the independent variable increases, so does the dependent variable. Where r is negative, this means that as the independent variable increases, the dependent variable decreases. The regression line would slope down from left to right. If I had used per cent Conservative as the dependent variable in the above example, that is what would have resulted.

The closer r is to +1 or –1, the stronger the relationship is; the closer it is to zero, the weaker the relationship. Values of +1 or –1 indicate absolutely perfect correlations. In that case all the points in a scatter diagram would be exactly on the regression line, and if we knew the independent variable score, we could calculate with complete accuracy the dependent variable score. Conversely, a correlation of 0 would mean that there was no (linear) relationship whatsoever between the two variables.

In practice, correlations of 1 or 0 are unheard of in electoral analysis. The illustration above produced a correlation coefficient of .90, which indicates a very strong relationship. (This is not a surprise since the fifteen constituencies were specifically selected to demonstrate a clear relationship.) For the same constituencies, the correlation between per cent Conservative and per cent working class is –.86 (a strong negative correlation) and when per cent Alliance is the dependent variable, the coefficient is –.32 (which is, given the small number of cases involved, a weak negative correlation).

I briefly noted above that we can measure the extent to which scores on variables are dispersed or concentrated by calculating the standard deviation. The square of the standard deviation (the standard deviation multiplied by itself) is called the *variance* and this is a measure of the amount of variation in a set of scores. An important feature of the correlation coefficient is that if it too is squared, then the resulting figure (r^2) is the proportion of the variation in the dependent variable that is statistically 'explained' or 'accounted for' by variations in the scores on the independent variable. Proportions are slightly cumbersome to handle and so they are normally converted to percentages by moving the decimal point two places to the right. Thus, the correlation between per cent working class and per cent Labour in our fifteen constituencies is .90, so $r^2 = .810$; that is, 81.0 per cent of the variation in the Labour vote in these seats is accounted for by variations in the size of the working class from one constituency to another. Similarly, variations in the per cent working class account for 74.0 per cent of the variation in the Conservative vote and for only 10.2 per cent of the variation in the Alliance vote.

This brief outline has attempted to explain in a simple way the principles underlying correlation and regression analysis and, although it is difficult to illustrate it visually, the same principles can be extended to analysis using two or more independent variables. This *multivariate* analysis enables numerous factors to be taken into account simultaneously by the use of what is called *multiple regression*. For example, to return to the fifteen constituencies I have used for illustration, we could add another independent variable to the analysis, say per cent owner-occupiers. We now know two things about each constituency in addition to the distribution of the vote. Does this improve our ability to account for variations in party support? As before, we can calculate regression equations and their associated r^2 statistics. In this case, with per cent Labour as the dependent variable the equation is

$$\% \text{ Labour} = -46.1 + 1.34 \ (\% \text{ working class}) + .16 \ (\% \text{ owner-occupiers})$$

The multiple r^2 is .830 so that 83 per cent of the variation in the Labour vote is accounted for by the two independent variables. Adding per cent owner-occupiers has increased our ability to predict the Labour vote by two percentage points. In principle, as many variables as desired can be added, but many will be found not to make any difference to the r^2 and can be discarded as not adding to the explanatory power of the equations. Much electoral analysis of this kind involves a search for a high r^2, which is frequently taken as a sign of analytical success.

Interpreting correlation coefficients

Correlation analysis is relatively easy to do (on a computer). Once the data are in a suitable form, it is simply a matter of punching them into the computer and calling up an appropriate programme. Correlation coefficients will then be churned out by the hundred in a few seconds. But care must be taken in interpreting these statistics, which are very frequently used in the literature on elections. Four important points should be borne in mind.

First, correlation does not equal causation. Just because two variables are strongly associated, it does not follow that one *causes* the other. Correlation tells us just what it says — the extent to which variables co-relate — nothing more and nothing less. Second, an associated point is that for a correlation to be of interest it must be of some theoretical significance. For all I know, there may be a strong correlation between the percentage of people in a constituency who have red hair and the size of the Liberal Democrat vote. But such a relationship would be virtually meaningless because there is no theory, hypothesis or suggestion as to why hair colour and party choice should be connected. The world is full of 'spurious' correlations, that is, phenomena that are statistically related but have absolutely no other conceivable connection. Third, correlations based on aggregate data tell us nothing about the behaviour of individuals. The fact that there is a strong positive correlation between the percentage of working-class people in a constituency and the percentage of the vote obtained by Labour *cannot* be used to infer that working-class people vote Labour. Although there may be a presumption that this is the case, all that can properly be inferred from the correlation is that the more working-class people there are, the higher is the Labour vote. We can draw conclusions about collectivities (constituencies), but not about the individuals who comprise them.[13] This distinction is very important. Inferring individual behaviour from aggregate statistics is known as the 'ecological fallacy' and is one of the most grievous sins that an electoral analyst can commit. Fourth, the absence of a high correlation coefficient does not mean that two variables are completely unrelated. Most correlation and regression analysis is concerned with linear (straight line) relationships but it is possible that variables may be related in other (curvilinear) ways. Without more advanced statistical techniques, the only way to check for non-linear patterns is by visual inspection of scatter diagrams.

Measuring electoral change

Thus far I have discussed the analysis of the results of a single election. This is sometimes called 'cross-sectional' analysis. But, of course, elections are held regularly in Britain — at least once every five years in the case of general elections and more frequently in the case of local elections. When a series of elections is brought into consideration, we immediately have a new set of dependent variables, namely *changes* in turn-out and in the distribution of votes from one election to another. In order to summarise changes in party support, psephologists have made much use of a measure known as 'swing'.

Swing was developed by Dr David Butler. It is simple to calculate and is defined as follows:

$$\frac{(C2 - C1) + (L1 - L2)}{2}$$

In this formula, C1 is the percentage share of the total vote obtained by the Conservatives at the first election and C2 the percentage at the second; L1 is Labour's share at the first election and L2 is Labour's percentage at the second. The statistic produced by this formula is known as 'Butler' or 'traditional' swing. By convention the parties are put in the order shown and the effect of this is that a positive figure denotes a swing to the Conservatives and a negative figure a swing to Labour. But the parties could appear in any order and any two parties could be substituted for Conservative and Labour.

A variant known as 'two-party' or 'Steed' swing (having been devised by Michael Steed) is also commonly used. Here the formula is exactly as above but, when calculating the percentage vote for the two parties concerned, votes for all other parties are excluded, so that the two parties' shares of the vote always total 100 per cent.

In the past, swing was a widely used and very useful measure of electoral change. It provided a simple summary of the extent of change and was used to compare inter-election movements in different parts of the country and in different constituencies. In addition, before general elections psephologists could work out the swing needed for any constituency to change hands. Thus, if a constituency had voted 54 per cent Conservative and 46 per cent Labour at the preceding election, then a swing to Labour of anything over 4 per cent would mean a Labour gain. Since swing tended to be in the same direction and of the same magnitude over the country as a whole, accurate estimates could be made of the number of seats that would change hands given a particular national swing and of the swing needed for a party to win or lose a majority of seats in the House of Commons.

These properties of swing enabled it to become the only statistical idea I know of that made someone a television personality. In the days before computer graphics, the late Robert McKenzie used to appear regularly on TV election programmes with a simple pendulum device which he called a 'swingometer'. When he moved it the appropriate number of points each way, it would show which seats were likely to change hands. The 'swingometer' was creaky but it was effective and certainly did a lot to educate the general public about the operation of elections and the electoral system in Britain.

The problem is that swing only works well if elections are essentially contests between two parties only. As Britain has moved to a situation in which patterns of party competition are much more complex, swing has lost its usefulness (see McAllister and Rose, 1984, ch. IX). There have been attempts to devise three-way swing figures but these are complicated to work out and lack the elegance and simplicity of traditional swing. The most common way of measuring aggregate or net electoral change nowadays is simply by calculating the changes in each party's percentage share of the vote.

These, like swing, are summary statistics. They do not tell us anything about how individuals behave, but rather describe the net effect of the changes in individuals' voting behaviour between two elections. This can be easily understood if we separate the different components of electoral change.

Whether over the country as a whole or in individual constituencies or wards (assuming no boundary changes), the differences between two consecutive election results are produced by four factors:

1. Switching between major parties. (For simplicity, I shall treat the Conservatives and Labour as the major parties.) Some people who voted Labour in the first election will vote Conservative in the second and vice versa. Clearly the outcome of the second election will only be affected if there is some imbalance in these switches.

2. Minor-party traffic. Here again party switching is involved but this time from minor parties (such as the Liberal Democrats, Greens, SNP) to one of the major parties and also to minor parties from one of the major parties. (There may also be some movement between different minor parties.) As with major-party switching, there will be some self-cancelling effect but an imbalance will affect the election outcome.

3. Non-voting traffic. Not everyone votes in every election. Some people who did not vote in the first election will vote in the second; others who voted first time round fail to do so the second time. Clearly, if one party's previous supporters stay away from the polls in larger numbers or if previous non-voters flock to one particular party, this will affect the result.

4. The physical replacement of the electorate. Every year (although the number fluctuates a little) around 750,000 people

in Britain reach 18 years of age, and therefore become eligible to vote, while about 650,000 people die. If one party gets a disproportionate share of the new voters or if the supporters of one party are dying off in greater numbers, this will affect election outcomes. Immigration to and emigration from the country or a particular constituency can have a similar effect. It is not unusual for population movement to change the character of a ward or constituency completely over time.

Aggregate measures of electoral change, such as swing, simply summarise the effects of all of these ebbs and flows. For more detailed information about the various components of change we have to turn to individual-level data produced by surveys.

Ideally, a survey study designed to analyse electoral change would interview a sample of voters after one election and then re-interview the same 'panel' after a second election. This minimises the chance of respondents misremembering how they voted in a previous election which may have been held as many as five years before. It is, of course, not possible to re-interview people who have died between the two elections and it is difficult to identify respondents who are too young to vote in the first election but who reach voting age by the time of the second.

None the less, when a survey obtains the reported votes of respondents at two successive elections the components of electoral change can be investigated by constructing a two-way table showing exactly what people did at the two elections. A table of this kind is sometimes called an 'election transition matrix' or, more simply, a 'flow of the vote' table, and Table 1.5 is an example.[14] In this case, the percentages shown are based on the total number of respondents in the table rather than on the number in each column.

Between the elections of 1987 and 1992, in the United Kingdom as a whole, the changes in the main parties' shares of the votes were: Conservative –0.4 per cent, Labour +3.6 per cent, Liberal Democrats –4.7 per cent. These figures suggest considerable stability in voting choice. By considering the survey evidence in Table 1.5, however, we can see that this net result was a product of considerable movement among voters — much of it self-cancelling. Thus, about 2 per cent of the electorate switched from

Table 1.5   Flow of the vote, 1987–92 (%).

| Vote in 1992 | Vote in 1987 | | | | |
	Con.	Lab.	Lib. Dem.	Non-voter	Too young
Con.	33	1	2	3	2
Lab.	2	23	1	2	2
Lib. Dem.	3	2	7	2	1
Non-voter	3	2	1	5	2
(Total N = 2,629)					

Note: Cell percentages are of the total number of respondents. The table is not a complete transition matrix since it excludes 'other' party voters as well as those who died between the elections.

Source: BES 1992 cross-section survey.

the Conservatives to Labour and 3 per cent from the Conservatives to the Liberal Democrats, but this was partly compensated by the fact that 3 per cent switched from these parties to the Conservatives. In terms of the components of change, these (incomplete) figures suggest that about 3 per cent of the electorate switched major parties between 1987 and 1992, 8 per cent were involved in third-party traffic, 13 per cent in non-voting traffic and 7 per cent were new voters. In total, almost a third of the 1992 electorate did not vote for the same party in both 1987 and 1992.

Clearly, then, aggregate measures of change between elections, while important and necessary, are limited. A fuller understanding of electoral change requires the kind of detailed information about individuals that only surveys can provide.[15]

Aggregate and survey data compared

Aggregate and survey data are both extensively used in electoral analysis and both have advantages and drawbacks. The advantages of using aggregate data are as follows:

1. If it is confined to publicly available data, it is cheap. It costs thousands of pounds to employ a firm to undertake a national survey of the British electorate. Even a modest local survey is expensive. In contrast, anyone can go to a library and

collect election results, census data and the like and then, armed only with a small calculator and a knowledge of some elementary statistical techniques, embark upon analysis.

2. Aggregate data such as election results reflect real behaviour — what voters actually did — while surveys only report what voters *say* they have done. There is sometimes a disjunction between these. Surveys always find, for instance, that more people claim to have voted in an election than actually did, according to the election returns.

3. Aggregate data usually refer to the total population being studied and are therefore not susceptible to sampling error in the way that survey data are.

4. Aggregate data are almost always interval-scale data and are suitable for analysing with the most powerful statistical techniques.

5. Survey studies of electoral behaviour are of relatively recent origin whereas lots of relevant aggregate data — in particular election results — are available, going back to the nineteenth century.

On the other hand, surveys also have important advantages.

1. Whereas with aggregate data we are usually restricted to material that has been collected and published — there are, for example, no official figures showing the distribution of different religions in British constituencies — in surveys the investigator can ask for any information that seems appropriate.

2. More precisely, aggregate statistics refer only to the objective characteristics and behaviour of a population. It is only by using surveys that the beliefs, attitudes and opinions of voters can be discovered.

3. Most important of all, however, individual data collected by survey permit analysis of individuals rather than collectivities. I have already commented on the importance of this with respect to electoral change, but it is of more general significance in electoral analysis. Without surveys we would not know which groups vote for which parties and in what proportions, and our theories about why people vote the way they do would be highly speculative.

My purpose in this chapter has not been to provide a comprehensive introduction to statistics. Rather it has been to familiarise those who know little about such matters with some of the statistical terms, measures and techniques which proliferate in the election literature. This should have made the literature somewhat more accessible to the non-specialist and provided a foundation for understanding the substantive material considered in subsequent chapters.

Notes

1. This was the number of UK constituencies at the 1992 general election. The boundaries of constituencies are currently being reviewed and it is unlikely that there will be the same number at the next election.
2. Comprehensive details of local election results in England and Wales have been published for each year since 1988, however, in a series of *Local Elections Handbooks* by Colin Rallings and Michael Thrasher of the University of Plymouth. John Bochel and David Denver have published a *Scottish Local Election Results* series, covering all elections since 1974. In addition, Rallings and Thrasher have collected all English and Welsh results in computerised form and deposited these at the ESRC Data Archive at the University of Essex.
3. There is a third scale of measurement — the ordinal scale — which I have ignored. Ordinal data are rarely analysed differently from the other two kinds.
4. Almost all elementary textbooks on statistics in social science do this. See, for example, Startup and Whittaker (1982).
5. 'Exit' polls involve interviewing voters as they leave the polling station after having voted.
6. See Gallup (1992).
7. See, for example, Worcester (1992).
8. Having said that, numbers are not given in many of the tables in later chapters for the sake of clarity of presentation since this is intended as an introductory text.
9. Dunleavy and Husbands (1985, p. 133) have a table showing vote by trade union membership, gender and social class in which percentages are based on numbers ranging from 14 to 77.
10. The constituencies are Barnsley West & Penistone, Basildon, Bethnal Green & Stepney, Brighton Kemptown, Chichester, Darlington, Epping Forest, Esher, Gloucester, Guildford, Makerfield, Milton Keynes, Nottingham East, Pudsey and Salford East. The figures for per cent working class are taken from Butler and Kavanagh (1988).
11. Technically it is the sum of the *squares* of the distance that is set at a minimum and the line is known as the 'least squares' line.

12. Anyone who doubts that this equation inevitably produces a straight line can check it very simply. Assign any values at all to a and b and then calculate the value of y for different values of x. For example, if a = 2 and b = 4, then when $x = 1$, $y = 2 + 4 (1) = 6$; when $x = 2$, $y = 2 + 4 (2) = 10$, and so on. If the x and y values are plotted against one another it will be found that they fall in a straight line.

13. In this example, for instance, it might be the case that in all constituencies a similar minority of working-class people vote Labour, but as the per cent working class increases, a larger proportion of *middle-class* people vote Labour. This would have the effect of producing a positive correlation between per cent working class and per cent Labour.

14. Fuller examples of election transition matrices, including estimates of the population entering and leaving the electorate, are given in Butler and Stokes (1974, ch. 12), Sarlvik and Crewe (1983, ch. 2) and Heath *et al.* (1991, ch. 2).

15. Details of the different components of swing for pairs of elections between 1959 and 1987 can be found in Heath *et al.* (1991, pp. 18, 26–8).

2

THE ERA OF ALIGNMENT 1950-70

The British general election of 1945 took place in very unusual circumstances. It was the first general election for ten years, the country was still at war with Japan and very many voters were serving in the Forces overseas (almost three million electors were registered as service voters). Given these circumstances, the best starting point for a review of post-war elections and electoral behaviour is not 1945 but 1950, the year of the first 'normal' post-war general election.

In this chapter, I consider the results of survey studies of voting between 1950 and 1970 and suggest that this period can be characterised as one of 'aligned' voting. First, however, it is necessary to look briefly at early American work in the field, since this had a major impact on voting research in Britain.

Two models of voting behaviour

Survey-based studies of voting behaviour in Britain in the 1950s and 1960s — and right up to today — have been very much influenced by theories, models and methods developed in the United States. Two major approaches have been influential.

The first, which might be called the 'social determinism' approach, emphasised the way in which party choice appeared to be an almost automatic consequence of a voter's social characteristics. The authors of the first-ever survey study of American voting behaviour, *The People's Choice* (Lazarsfeld, Berelson and Gaudet, 1968, 1st edn. 1944), had intended to focus upon short-term factors affecting voting choice in the presidential election of 1940 — the book was subtitled 'How the voter makes up his mind in a presidential campaign' — but they became more impressed by the importance of social characteristics such as class and religion. Lazarsfeld and his colleagues discovered that they could predict a person's vote with considerable accuracy from knowledge of just a few social characteristics. They concluded that 'a person thinks, politically, as he is socially. Social characteristics determine political preference' (p. 27).

Describing relationships between various social and demographic characteristics and party choice — while always interesting — is not, however, in itself very useful. It would certainly be interesting if it were found that left-handed people with brown eyes tended to vote in a distinctive way but it seems unlikely that knowing this will advance our understanding of what motivates voters. What is required is some theory that explains why there should be a link between specific social characteristics and voting. We need an answer to the question 'Why should some social differences be associated with political differences whereas others should not?'

In 1948, the authors of *The People's Choice* carried out a second study and in *Voting* (Berelson, Lazarsfeld and McPhee, 1954) they extended and reinforced their original argument. In particular, they provided an answer to the above question by suggesting that for a social difference to be translated into a political cleavage, three conditions need to be fulfilled. These are as follows:

> (1) initial social differentiation such that the consequences of political policy are materially or symbolically different for different groups; (2) conditions of transmittibility from generation to generation; and (3) conditions of physical and social proximity providing for continued in-group contact in succeeding generations. (p. 75)

The first condition requires that the social groups concerned must have differing material or symbolic interests which are affected by government policy. Thus council tenants and owner-occupiers might have different interests with regard to housing policy. Policy in areas like abortion or embryo research might not directly affect many people but could be said to be of symbolic importance to some groups such as Roman Catholics and others. On the other hand, 'groups' such as the left-handed or the red-headed are not normally treated differently from the rest of the population in matters of public policy and do not fulfil the first condition. The second and third conditions relate to the processes by which social and political divisions are maintained and reinforced.

We have here, then, what might be termed an 'interests plus socialisation' theory or model. Different social groups have different interests and hence different needs. They therefore tend to vote for different parties which they perceive as representing these interests. Awareness of a group's distinctiveness and of group-party links is sustained by regular contact with fellow group members in the family, among peers and in the community.

This is an appealing and apparently simple model but it is not without difficulties. Very briefly, four problems with the model are as follows:

1. Overlapping group memberships. Everyone belongs to a variety of social groups and the theory offers no clues as to which will be decisive in determining an individual's party support and why.
2. Group interests. It is not self-evident that a large and relatively heterogeneous group of people will have the same interests. Who decides what the group's interests are, and in what sense can political parties be said to represent group interests?
3. Deviants. How does the model account for the (often large) minorities who do not conform to group voting norms?
4. Political parties. The theory tends to give the impression that party choice is a sort of spontaneous effect of social location and ignores the active role that political parties play in mobilising and structuring the electorate.

Despite criticisms of this kind, some form of 'social determinism' underpinned by the idea of 'interests plus socialisation' has heavily influenced voting research in Britain.

The second major American influence on British voting studies derives from a book called *The American Voter* (Campbell, Converse, Miller and Stokes, 1960). In this profoundly influential study Campbell and his colleagues developed a model of voting behaviour which has come to be known as the 'Michigan model', since the original research was directed from the University of Michigan. Like the 'social determinism' model, the Michigan model suggests that long-term factors are most important in determining party choice. But there is not a simple step from social location to voting behaviour. Rather, the social position that an individual occupies affects the kinds of influences that he or she will encounter in interacting with family, friends, neighbours, workmates and so on. As a consequence of these interactions — especially within the family — the individual acquires a *party identification*. This means a sense of attachment to a party, a feeling of commitment to it, being a supporter of the party — rather like being an Everton supporter or a Partick Thistle supporter — and not just someone who happens to vote for the party from time to time.

When there is an election, there is an interaction between a voter's long-term party identification and various short-term influences, such as current political issues, campaign events, the personalities of party leaders or candidates and, we might add, the tactical situation in the local constituency, to produce a vote decision. The Michigan team were at pains to emphasise, however, that it is the long-term factors that are usually decisive. Indeed a person's party identification will influence how he or she interprets and evaluates issues, party leaders and so on.

The concept of party identification is central to the Michigan model and it is worth exploring it in a little more detail. It is important to grasp that identifying with a party is not the same as voting for it. Indeed it is possible to identify with one party and vote for a different one. This happens frequently in American presidential elections. President Reagan's electoral success was largely due to his ability to get Democratic party identifiers to vote for him, even though he was a Republican and these 'Reagan Democrats' continued to support the Democratic party in Congressional and other elections. But the same sort of thing happens in Britain. A Labour supporter living in a constituency in which Labour has no realistic chance of winning — Chelmsford, for example — might decide to vote Liberal Democrat while still remaining basically a Labour supporter.

There are three clear differences between party identification and voting. First, party identification is psychological while voting is behavioural. That is, identification exists in people's heads; we

cannot observe it directly. Voting, however, is a definite action —
putting a cross on a piece of paper or pulling a lever on a voting
machine — and it is, in principle, observable (although normally
done in secret). Second, voting is time-specific while party identification is not. Voting can only take place at an election — and
elections occur relatively infrequently in Britain — whereas identification is ongoing and continuous. There does not need to be an
election in the offing for people to consider themselves supporters
of a party. Third, party identification varies in intensity and voting
does not. Some people will be very strong party supporters, others
not very strong or just weak supporters. All votes count equally,
however, whether the voter marks the ballot with a large bold
black cross or a tiny faint one.

Party identification is, then, distinct from voting. This means that
it can be used to help explain party choice in an election, as in the
Michigan model. According to the theory, party identification
serves important functions for the individual. It simplifies the task
of understanding the complex world of politics. Once someone
decides (or has learned) who are the 'goodies' and who the 'bad-
dies' in the party battle, there is no need to pay great attention to
the details of political debate, no need to bother with the details of
party policies or election manifestos. Identification also acts as a
sort of psychological filter or prism through which political messages pass to the individual; it provides a framework within which
political events are understood and evaluated.

When party identification is widespread, it has important effects
on the political system as a whole. Most obviously it provides an
element of stability and continuity. (Everton supporters do not
suddenly switch their affections to Liverpool or Manchester
United, and it is much the same with political parties.) If people
identify with a party they are not likely to shoot off in all directions
at successive elections. Rather, they will have a 'normal' vote
which in most cases will remain stable from election to election.

Aligned voting in Britain 1950–70

When these approaches were applied to Britain in the 1950s and
1960s, a clear picture of the British electorate emerged. This is summarised in Figure 2.1. Broadly speaking, the electorate was divided

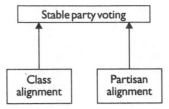

Figure 2.1   Aligned voting in Britain.

into two large blocs which provided reliable and stable voting support for the Conservative and Labour parties. The interconnected phenomena of class and partisan alignment were the twin pillars, as it were, which supported and sustained stable party support on the part of individual voters and a stable two-party system overall.

Partisan alignment

By partisan alignment I mean a situation in which voters align themselves with a party by thinking of themselves as supporters of it, by having a party identification. This was certainly the case in Britain in the 1950s and 1960s. The standard survey question designed to elicit the kind of generalised psychological commitment implied by party identification is: 'Generally speaking, do you think of yourself as Conservative, Labour, Liberal Democrat or what?' Surveys at the three elections between 1964 and 1970 found that the overwhelming majority of voters were willing to nominate a party that they supported and of those, most nominated the Labour or Conservative parties (see Table 2.1).

It is possible that the survey question normally used does not in fact tap the kind of enduring, deep-rooted commitment which is implied by the concept of party identification, but that voters respond by simply naming the party that they currently favour. This possibility has been considered by, among others, Butler and Stokes (1974, pp. 39–47) and Crewe, Sarlvik and Alt (1977, pp. 139–42). Both showed that voters were much more likely to change their vote without changing identification than to change their identification without changing their vote, and concluded on this basis that the question 'works' and that party identification

Table 2.1 Party identification, 1964–70 (%).

	1964	*1966*	*1970*
With party identification	92	90	89
With Conservative or Labour identification	81	80	81
'Very strong' identifiers	43	43	41
'Very strong' Conservative or Labour identifiers	40	39	40

Source: Sarlvik and Crewe (1983, pp. 334–5).

really did exist among voters. Indeed, more recent research suggests that these earlier studies may have underestimated the extent of 'genuine' party identification in Britain for technical reasons related to the order in which the voting and party identification questions have been asked in surveys (see Heath and Pierce, 1992). We can conclude, then, as Butler and Stokes put it, that in the 1960s 'millions of British electors remain anchored to one of the parties for very long periods of time. Indeed many electors have had the same party loyalties from the dawn of their political consciousness' (p. 47). Common experience confirms that party identification still exists. We all know people who are 'Conservatives' or 'Labour supporters' rather than people who just happen to vote Conservative or Labour at a specific election.

As a standard follow-up to the party identification question in election surveys, respondents are asked how strongly Conservative or Labour (or whatever) they feel. People can be characterised as 'very strong' identifiers, 'fairly strong' or 'not very strong'. In the three surveys reported in Table 2.1, more than two-fifths of the electorate were prepared to describe themselves as 'very strong' party supporters and almost all of these were Conservative or Labour identifiers.

Strength of party identification has important effects upon electoral behaviour. Stronger identifiers are more likely to turn out to vote, to vote for the party with which they identify, and to be stable in their party choice over time, than are weaker identifiers. The latter are more likely to make their minds up about who to vote for closer to election day itself, rather than well in advance of it, and to be more 'wobbly' in the sense of seriously considering voting for a party other than their eventual choice. I shall return to these important differences in later chapters.

Clearly, then, a partisan alignment existed in Britain during this period. The extent and strength of commitment to the Conservative and Labour parties provided a basis for stability in electoral behaviour and for a two-party system that seemed secure.

Class alignment

Between 1950 and 1970, of all the possible social characteristics that might have influenced party choice, social class was consistently found to be the most important. Generally, about two-thirds of working-class voters supported the Labour party and upwards of four-fifths of the 'solid' middle class voted Conservative. Writing in 1967, Peter Pulzer concluded, in a much-quoted sentence, that 'Class is the basis of British party politics; all else is embellishment and detail' (1967, p. 98). Similarly, on the basis of figures such as those given in Table 2.2, Butler and Stokes reported:

> Our findings on the strength of links between class and partisanship in Britain echo broadly those of every other opinion poll or voting study . . . there were strong enough cross-currents in each class for partisanship not to have been determined entirely by class. Yet its pre-eminent role can hardly be questioned. (1974, p. 77)

There was a clear alignment between class and party. Britain was, indeed, considered the archetypal class-based party system. At this point, however, we need to pause for a moment to consider what exactly 'class' is and how it is measured.

Table 2.2 Party self-image by occupational class, 1963 (%).

	Higher mana-gerial	Lower mana-gerial	Super-visory non-manual	Lower non-manual	Skilled manual	Unskilled manual
Conservative	87	81	77	61	29	25
Labour	14	19	23	39	71	75

Note: The table is restricted to respondents with a Conservative or Labour 'self-image', which is the term used by Butler and Stokes to denote identification.
Source: Butler and Stokes (1974, p. 78).

Defining class

Despite its central position in voting behaviour research, the concept of class is slippery and difficult to define precisely. It is even more difficult to measure or 'operationalise' in empirical research.

When we say that a person is 'middle class' or 'working class' we often have a variety of things in mind — wealth, income, occupation, education, accent, 'style of life' and so on. So how is a person's class to be determined? Generally, voting researchers, as well as opinion pollsters and market researchers, have opted for occupation as a short-hand indicator of class. This can be justified on the grounds that most people describe different classes in terms of different occupations (see Butler and Stokes, 1974, p. 70) but it also gives rise to other problems. How many classes are there? Which occupations belong to which classes? The classes of bank managers and coal miners may be fairly obvious, but what about typists, policemen or foremen on building sites? Is a self-employed plumber in a different class from a plumber who is employed by a large firm?

Another set of problems relates to the categorisation of women. Should employed married women be classified according to their own job or the job of their husbands (the reasoning being that the husband is traditionally the 'head of the household' and thus determines the whole family's status)? And what about married women who are full-time housewives and mothers?

Clearly, the definition and measurement of this most basic social variable is fraught with difficulty. Indeed, as we shall see in Chapter 3, the very definition of class came to be an important element in the debate, which has taken place among academics over the past ten years or so, concerning trends in the level of class voting in Britain.

Opinion polling firms have developed comprehensive schemes for coding (or classifying) occupations into five main groups whose names have become familiar to poll-watchers. These are as follows:

A Higher professional, managerial and administrative.
B Intermediate professional, managerial and administrative.
C1 Supervisory, clerical and other non-manual.
C2 Skilled manual.

D   Semi- and unskilled manual.

E   Residual, casual workers, people reliant on state benefits.

Voting researchers frequently combine these into two groups — non-manual workers (ABC1) and manual workers (C2DE). This is partly for purely practical reasons. If a survey uses a fivefold categorisation, the number of respondents in each class will be smaller than with a dichotomous scheme and detailed analysis will be inhibited. Partly also the reality is that most people do seem to think of the British class structure in terms of a basic division between a middle and a working class. Nevertheless, it should be borne in mind that the manual/non-manual distinction is a very rough and ready approximation to what we mean when we talk about social class.

Other social influences on voting

Although class was the dominant source of political alignment in Britain in the 1950s and 1960s, other social and demographic characteristics were also consistently found to be associated with party choice. Two preliminary points about these relationships should be noted. First, the importance of class as a determinant of voting was such that for any other variable to be shown to have an effect, it had to have such an effect when class was 'controlled' (see Chapter 1). There would, for example, be little point in getting excited over a finding that most Roman Catholics voted Labour if it were also the case that most Roman Catholics were working class. Second, while the job of establishing the existence of positive relationships between social attributes and party choice is relatively straightforward, explaining them is not. Voting researchers might agree about which groups vote for which parties but that does not mean that they are in agreement about why they do so.

Age

There is a well-known aphorism, the origins of which are obscure, which goes something like this: 'If you're not a radical at 20 you've no heart; if you're not a conservative at 60 you've no head.' The precise ages referred to vary a lot but the general sentiment of this

Table 2.3   Conservative lead over Labour by age and class, 1964–70.

Election	1964		1966		1970	
Age	Under 35	54+	Under 35	54+	Under 35	54+
Professional/managerial	32	84	36	68	6	60
Intermediate non-manual	25	45	5	37	2	42
Manual working class	–43	–31	–49	–36	–22	–9

Note: The figure in each cell is % Conservative minus % Labour among the class/ age group concerned.
Source: Calculated from table 1.15 in Crewe, Day and Fox (1991).

piece of folk-wisdom is clear enough and it appeared to find empirical support from voting studies in the 1950s and 1960s. Academic surveys and opinion polls regularly found that younger people, especially the youngest age group in the electorate, were more inclined to vote Labour while older voters favoured the Conservatives.

Summary figures for a younger and an older age group are shown in Table 2.3. In every class group, at each of the three elections the Conservative lead is much greater or the Labour lead smaller among older voters. When age groups are broken down further, the way in which Conservative support relative to Labour steadily increases as we move up the age groups is even more obvious (see, for example, Rose, 1974, p. 521). It is clear that within each class there is an age effect. What is not clear is why this should be so.

Two main explanations have been offered. The first suggests what is called a 'lifecycle' effect and is essentially the explanation implicit in the aphorism quoted above. Young people tend to be idealistic and to favour social and political change. As they grow older, however, people acquire more responsibilities, more of a stake in society (such as property) and become more aware of the difficulties associated with rapid social change. They thus become more cautious and conservative in outlook.

The second explanation concentrates on political generations or 'cohorts'. In this view, it is not so much a person's chronological age that is important as when he or she was young and beginning to experience politics. As each generation enters the electorate it is influenced by currently decisive political events — the Vietnam

War in the 1960s, for example, or the 'winter of discontent' in 1978/9 — or, more broadly, 'the nature of the times'. Thus, people voting for the first time in 1945 would have been influenced by having lived through a war and the strongly pro-Labour feeling in the country at that time. Their political attitudes and behaviour would continue to be influenced by this for a long time. Using the idea of political generations, the strength of Conservative support among older people in Britain in the 1950s and 1960s could be explained by the fact that anyone aged over 60 in, say, 1964 would have come of age in the 1920s or before, when Labour was a relatively new party. Their earliest influences, therefore, were unlikely to have been in a pro-Labour direction.

As in so many cases, there is something to be said for both of these views. Generally, however, the data — including data from other countries in which increasing age is also associated with increasing conservatism — are more supportive of the 'life cycle' rather than the generational approach. The tendency for Labour support to be weaker among older age groups persists as different generations move through the electorate.

Sex

Like age, a person's sex is not usually too difficult to discover and classify.[1] In this case too, in the 1950s and 1960s there was a regular pattern: men were less likely to vote Conservative and more likely to vote Labour than women. As Pulzer (1967, p. 107) put it:

> There is overwhelming evidence that women are more Conservatively inclined than men . . . sex is the one factor which indubitably counter-balances class trends: working-class women are more right-wing than working-class men, middle-class women are more right-wing than middle-class men.

Table 2.4, which again uses BES data, illustrates this. Although the differences are neither as large nor as consistent as those found for age, the general pattern is clear. By controlling for class, the possibility that women are more Conservative because they are more likely to have non-manual occupations is excluded. What is not excluded, however, is the possibility that the apparent sex difference is actually an age difference, since women live longer than

Table 2.4 Conservative lead over Labour by sex and class, 1964–70.

| Election | 1964 | | 1966 | | 1970 | |
Sex	Male	Female	Male	Female	Male	Female
Professional/managerial	48	56	47	46	36	45
Intermediate non-manual	30	33	19	34	23	23
Manual working class	−39	−34	−48	−41	−29	−16

Note: The figure in each cell is % Conservative minus % Labour among the sex/age group concerned.

Source: Calculated from table 1.14 in Crewe, Day and Fox (1991).

men. There is, however, no shortage of other hypotheses to explain the greater Conservatism of women in this period. It can be argued, for instance, that women in working-class families have traditionally been more home-centred than men. While men went out to work, women stayed at home to look after children. This insulated them from industrial conflicts and wider community pressures. It may be also that women are more likely than men to be the bearers of traditional values, relating to religion and the family for example, and this makes them more conservative. It has even been suggested that women are more socially aspiring than men, which is why they also have more 'genteel' and less strongly regional accents.[2]

Religion

The following incident is recorded in Butler and Stokes' discussion of religious affiliation and party choice:

> One of our interviewers recorded a colloquy with a respondent who said 'none' in answer to her initial question about religious affiliation. She then inquired, on her own initiative, whether she ought to put him down as 'atheist' or 'agnostic'. The respondent thereupon asked to be told the difference between the two ... After hearing her account, the respondent said, 'You had better put me down as Church of England.' (1974, pp. 156–7)

This illustrates very well the difficulty of classifying voters according to religious denomination and of analysing the relationship between religion and party choice. The respondent presumably *was* put down as C of E and incorporated into the analysis on that

Table 2.5   Party self-image by religion and class, 1963 (%).

	Middle Class				Working Class			
	C. of Eng.	C. of Scot.	Non-conformist	RC	C. of Eng.	C. of Scot.	Non-conformist	RC
Con.	72	74	41	55	30	25	22	18
Lab.	10	22	22	26	55	59	62	68
Lib.	18	4	37	19	15	16	16	14

Source: Butler and Stokes (1974, p. 158).

basis. In a largely secular, non-churchgoing society it is not clear what it means to say that someone 'belongs' to one religious denomination or another.

None the less, in many Western European states religion remains a highly important determinant of party choice. And the same was true of Britain in the late nineteenth and early twentieth centuries. In those days, the Church of England could fairly be described as 'the Tory party at prayer' while the Liberal party was strongly supported by Nonconformists. Religious issues, such as support for established church schools from the rates (local taxes) or the question of the disestablishment of the Anglican church in Wales, excited much political passion.[3]

By the 1950s and 1960s, however, the influence of religion on political party choice, although still in evidence (and of paramount importance in Northern Ireland), had greatly declined. Table 2.5 shows that middle-class Anglicans were more likely to support the Conservative party than were Nonconformists or Roman Catholics, and that working-class Nonconformists and Roman Catholics were more strongly Labour. The relatively strong support for the Liberals among middle-class Nonconformists is also clear. Butler and Stokes, from whom this table is taken, do not give figures for people who have no religious affiliation but other evidence shows that this group was inclined to support Labour (for a fuller discussion see Bochel and Denver, 1970).

Explanations for the association between religion and party in Britain have tended to focus on the fact that the Church of England, as the established church, is identified with the social and political establishment, while religious dissent goes hand in hand with political dissent. Catholics in Britain are to a considerable extent descendants of Irish immigrants, and for them the Conservatives are identified as the party which had vigorously opposed Irish Home Rule and supported Ulster Protestants in forcing the partition of Ireland in 1922.

As this point illustrates, the influence of religion on party choice in the 1950s and 1960s was very much a legacy of past struggles. Butler and Stokes were convinced that it was a legacy that was steadily disappearing. Only in Northern Ireland itself, and in parts of mainland Britain where the Irish influence remained strong, did religion appear to continue to have a powerful impact on party choice.

Region and locality

In analysing regional voting patterns, students of elections have generally made use of the 'standard regions' defined by the Registrar General's Office for census and other purposes. In this definition, England is divided into eight regions — the North, Yorkshire and Humberside, East Midlands, East Anglia, South East, South West, West Midlands and the North West — while Scotland, Wales and Northern Ireland are also defined as standard regions. Dividing up the country in this way is inevitably rather arbitrary and it is unlikely that everyone living in these regions feels a distinctive regional identity (except, of course, Scotland, Wales and Northern Ireland where people would resent the use of the term 'region'). People living in Newcastle-upon-Tyne, for example, would consider themselves 'Geordies' rather than inhabitants of the North region.

None the less, despite the artificiality of official regional boundaries, elections in the 1950s and 1960s were marked by very clear regional voting patterns which were reproduced in election after election. Indeed, Rose (1974, p. 490) demonstrates that these regional patterns stretch right back to 1918 with very little alteration. Very broadly, Britain was divided into 'two nations' electorally. Labour support was higher and Conservative support lower in Scotland, Wales and Northern England than in the rest of England.[4]

To some extent, this pattern reflected differences in the social composition of the electorate. Since there were (and are) more working-class people in Scotland, Wales and the North than elsewhere, Labour would be expected to do better anyway. But even

Table 2.6   Party support by region and class, 1963–66 (%).

| | Scotland, Wales and North | | South and Midlands | |
	Middle class	Working class	Middle class	Working class
Conservative	70	30	75	37
Labour	30	70	25	63

Note: The table is restricted to Conservative and Labour supporters only.
Source: Butler and Stokes (1974, p. 129).

when class is controlled, regional differences persist. Table 2.6 shows how people of different classes voted in the mid-1960s within two broad regional groupings. As can be seen, within both classes the Conservative share of the vote is larger and Labour's smaller in the South and Midlands.

This table is restricted to Conservative and Labour voters only, and it gives no information about two other distinctively regional features of elections during this period. The first was the distribution of support for the Liberals, which was markedly higher than average in the South West of England and in rural parts of Scotland and Wales. This continued the reputation of the Liberals as the party of the 'Celtic fringe'. Second, in the late 1960s there was an upsurge of political nationalism in Scotland and Wales, with the nationalist parties (SNP and Plaid Cymru) significantly increasing their support. This further heightened the electoral distinctiveness of these two countries.

Explaining regional variations in voting behaviour in Britain is a complex task and I shall return to it in Chapter 6 when I discuss post-1970 election trends. For the moment, it is worth re-emphasising that distinctive regional voting has existed for over seventy years. This suggests that an adequate explanation will not be found by pointing to the regional effects of the policies of particular governments. Clearly, there is something more deep-seated and enduring at work. It is difficult, however, to be specific about what this something might be. Analysts often have to invoke rather vague ideas like distinctive social, religious and political traditions or distinctive cultures to explain regional electoral differentiation.

Centre–periphery theory perhaps provides a less vague general explanation (see Steed, 1986). Put simply, this theory argues that British society, like some other societies, is divided into a centre or core and a periphery. The centre, London and the South East in this case, dominates the periphery culturally, economically and politically. Peripheral regions are poorer, suffer more in times of economic depression, have worse housing conditions and so on. As a result they tend to favour radical, non-establishment parties. This theory certainly does not fit the British case perfectly but it does offer some clues to understanding the geographical pattern of voting in Britain.

Butler and Stokes (1974, pp. 120–7) took their analysis of regional variations in party support a stage further by looking at the influence of the particular locality where people live. They found that the social composition of the local community affected individuals' party choice. The more middle class an area was, then the more Conservative were both middle-class and working-class voters; the more working class an area, the more strongly Labour were both groups of voters. Thus a voter living in a town like St Helens, which is heavily working class, would be more likely to vote Labour than a voter of the same class living in, say, Southport. Voters, then, tend to conform to the locally dominant political norm. If almost everyone that one meets at work, in shops, pubs and clubs appears to support the same party, then there is strong pressure on an individual to support that party too. This is sometimes called a 'neighbourhood', 'contact' or 'contagion' effect and it is a phenomenon I shall also discuss further in Chapter 6.

Class, age, sex, religion and region were the five most important socio-demographic variables influencing the British voter during the era of alignment. Voting studies investigated and provided information on a host of other variables, of course — housing tenure, trade union membership, education, the urban–rural differences, car ownership and so on — but to a large extent, these can be seen as variations on the main themes provided by the five factors that I have looked at in some detail. It is worth noting, however, that race or ethnic group does not appear in the list I have given. This is because ethnic minorities constituted a tiny fraction of the electorate during this period and little attention was paid to their voting behaviour.

Explaining the 'deviants': working-class Tories

Although occupational class was the social characteristic most strongly related to party choice (or at least to the choice between Conservative and Labour) there were, of course, many people who 'crossed over' and voted for the party of the opposite class. How could such 'deviance' be explained? Although both middle-class Labour supporters and working-class Conservatives are of interest in this respect, by far the greatest attention has been paid to the latter group. This is because working-class Tories are numerically and historically a more important group. Throughout most of the twentieth century, the working class easily outnumbered the middle class and yet for lengthy periods Britain has been ruled by the Conservatives. They could not possibly have gained office without substantial working-class support, while Labour would never have been out of office if they had the support of the entire working class.

A number of explanations of working-class Conservatism have been put forward and in this section they are briefly summarised.

1. *Cross-pressures*. One line of explanation followed the pattern established in *Voting* (Berelson *et al.*, 1954). It emphasises the fact that working-class people are also members of other social groups — someone could be a working-class Anglican home-owner, for example — and suggests that if these other groups are Conservative-inclined, membership of them will cut across and attenuate the basic class identity of the individual. As a result, he or she will experience 'cross-pressures' and may consequently vote in a class-deviant way. The kind of conclusion to which this sort of analysis leads is illustrated (with tongue firmly in cheek) by Runciman who writes:

   > The ideal type of the working-class Conservative is a woman in her seventies, living in a country district in the Midlands, whose father was in a non-manual occupation, who stayed on at school beyond the minimum age, who thinks of herself as 'middle class', and who would like to attend regularly at an Anglican church but is prevented by age or illness from doing so. (1966, pp. 175–6)

   One problem with this kind of explanation is that it amounts to little more than an exercise in probability. If, for example,

60 per cent of people having some shared social characteristic (other than class) vote Conservative, then that is interpreted as a cleavage which cross-cuts being working class. Little guidance is offered as to why some people who are members of 'cross-cutting' groups should 'defect' from their class party while others do not.

2. *Misperception of class position*. Class, as I have suggested, is a complex phenomenon; and, although an individual may be assigned to a class by a researcher on the basis of some 'objective' characteristic such as occupation, it is frequently the case that the individual's 'subjective' view of his or her own class position is not the same as the objective categorisation. We have already seen evidence of the importance of this (Table 1.4). Runciman (1966, ch. IX) explored the question in some detail. He found (p. 186) that 'manual workers and their wives who describe themselves as "middle-class" and attach some orthodox meaning to this are consistently likelier to support the Conservative Party' and explained this in terms of reference-group theory. 'Self-rated' class was a better guide to party choice than objective class but this still leaves unexplained why some members of the objective working class should fail to identify with that class and why, even among the subjective working class, there was still considerable support for the Conservatives.

3. *Deference*. Two important book-length studies of working-class Conservatism (Nordlinger, 1967; McKenzie and Silver, 1968) reject explanations in terms of social and demographic differences within the working class, and concentrate upon attitudes — in particular, attitudes of deference. McKenzie and Silver measure deference by means of six tests and suggest that 'deferentials' are more likely to prefer political leaders of socially superior origins, to assess the relative merits of the parties primarily in terms of the personal qualities of their leaders, to interpret policies which benefit the working class as a consequence of the élite's goodwill or indulgence, to believe that the role of ordinary voters is to confirm the right of the traditional élite to govern, to accept uncritically the monarchy and the House of Lords and to evaluate the Conservative party as distinctly a 'national' party.

Working-class people who have these sorts of attitudes are predisposed to vote Conservative.

The concept of deference is difficult to operationalise in survey research and McKenzie and Silver's tests have been subject to criticism (see Kavanagh, 1971). In any case, both McKenzie and Silver and Nordlinger find that many working-class Conservatives do not share these attitudes and, in addition, that many Labour voters are just as deferential as Conservatives. This casts doubt on the validity of the claim that deferential attitudes explain working-class Conservatism. Both studies suggest, however, that even when they were undertaken, working-class deference was declining.

4. *Embourgeoisement.* After Labour lost its third election in a row in 1959, many commentators believed that Labour was losing out among the working class because of growing affluence. As they became more prosperous, workers began to acquire consumer durables (like washing machines and cars), to become owner-occupiers and to go abroad for their holidays. In other words, they were becoming more like the middle class, more bourgeois, and in consequence switching politically to the Conservatives.

The 'embourgeoisement thesis' was elaborated and tested among affluent workers in Luton in 1962 by John Goldthorpe and his colleagues (Goldthorpe, Lockwood, Bechhofer and Platt, 1968). (It is powerful testimony to the effects of inflation that a worker was deemed to be 'affluent' in 1962 if he earned £17 per week!) Goldthorpe *et al.* found that, contrary to the embourgeoisement thesis, affluent workers were *more* likely to be Labour supporters than were working-class people in general. They detected, however, a significant difference in the nature of the support given to Labour by affluent workers as compared with the traditional working class. Affluent workers voted Labour because they expected a Labour government to bring them direct benefits. Support was conditional and instrumental rather than 'solidaristic'. If Labour did not deliver the goods then their support would be withdrawn. Herein, perhaps, lay some of the seeds of the difficulties Labour was to encounter among working-class voters after 1970.

5. *Political generations.* I discussed earlier the idea of political generations or cohorts. Butler and Stokes (1974) use the idea to present an 'evolutionary' view of working-class Conservatism. In outline, the argument is that party loyalty is largely passed on from generation to generation within the family. The problem for Labour was that it was a relatively late arrival on the political scene — it was not a major national party until the 1920s. By then many families had already established patterns of support for other parties. Consequently, many people alive in the 1950s — especially older people — could not have been socialised into supporting Labour because their parents and grandparents (more precisely, fathers and grandfathers) had established their party loyalty before Labour was on the scene. Butler and Stokes note (p. 185) that six out of seven constituencies had never had a Labour candidate before 1918. Because of the importance of family socialisation, Conservative, or at least non-Labour, loyalties continued to be transmitted even after the emergence of Labour. There was, of course, some 'leakage' as the lines of transmission lengthened with the passage of time, and Butler and Stokes suggested that on this account working-class Conservatism would decline.

   This historical dimension to working-class Tory voting makes for a powerful and convincing argument — as far as the 1950s and 1960s are concerned. It is not clear that it can work for the 1970s and 1980s when the lines of transmission back to 1918 and before are very long indeed.

6. *Asking the wrong question.* The sociologist, Frank Parkin, in a well-known article turned the whole argument about working-class Tories on its head (Parkin, 1967). The problem was not, he argued, to explain why some working-class people voted Conservative but why anyone at all voted Labour! Parkin suggested that the dominant 'institutional, orders' of British society — such as private property, the monarchy, the mass media, the Established Church — embody values that are in accord with Conservatism and hostile to socialism. People exposed to these dominant or core values would be expected to vote Conservative. People can only resist this psychological pressure if they are protected, as it were, by subcultures formed within working-class communities, trade unions or large factories.

This is certainly an interesting way to look at the problem. Clearly, however, Parkin's analysis is less empirically based than the other explanations and it depends upon some large assumptions about the nature of the dominant value system and the connections between generalised values and electoral behaviour.

Conclusion

In Figure 2.1 I summarised the picture of the British electorate that emerged from voting studies in the 1950s and 1960s. As a result of class and partisan alignment, voters were divided into two blocs which could be relied upon to turn out in election after election to support their party. Figure 2.2 represents how the individual voter was thought of as coming to make his or her decision at elections.

The starting point of the model is the class and party of voters' parents and it is underlain by the theory of political socialisation. Butler and Stokes saw party identification as inherited, to a large extent, through the family and in support of their position presented the data shown in Table 2.7. Where both parents had supported a major party, three-quarters or more of Butler and Stokes' respondents supported the same party. Later critics have cast doubt on the way in which Butler and Stokes used and

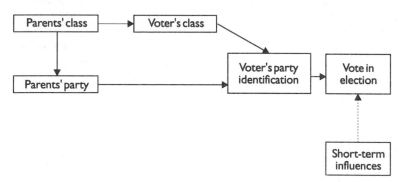

Figure 2.2   The aligned voter.

Table 2.7   The influence of parents' partisanship on party identification, 1963 (%).

	Both parents Conservative	Parents divided	Both parents Labour
No party identification	3	4	3
Conservative	75	37	10
Labour	14	49	81
Liberal	8	10	6

Note: 'Divided' means that one parent was Conservative and the other Labour.
Source: Butler and Stokes (1974, p. 52).

interpreted these data (see Rose and McAllister, 1990, pp. 46–8) — the table excludes voters who do not know or cannot remember how their parents voted, for example, but it is consistent with the general model put forward by Butler and Stokes.

The representation or model described in Figure 2.2 is, of course, highly simplified. But it emphasises the long-term forces of class and party identification, both of which were to a large extent inherited. The significance of this was such that it made little sense to think of the voter as 'deciding' to vote for one party or another in an election. Rather the voter had a 'standing decision' or commitment to a party, and voting for it in elections was nearly automatic. The model does not, of course, describe the voting behaviour of every single elector. As we have seen, not everyone supported their 'natural' class party and some did not identify with a party. There were always 'floating' voters who switched parties in successive elections. None the less, Figure 2.2 is the best simple representation of how the party choice of the average voter was thought to be determined in the era of alignment.

This raises a problem, however. If voting behaviour was so stable how can we account for electoral change? In the short term, between pairs of elections, if this model were accurate we would expect little change. If we think in terms of an election transition matrix, the majority of voters would fall in the cells on the diagonal from top left to bottom right.

Table 2.8 summarises electoral change between three pairs of elections. On each occasion about two-thirds of respondents were in these cells, and most of those who were not drifted between voting and non-voting, which is also consistent with the model. Only small minorities of voters actually switched parties. None the

Table 2.8   Constancy and change between pairs of elections, 1959–70 (%).

	1959–64	1964–66	1966–70
Voted Con. or Lab. twice	51	55	47
Voted Lib. or minor party twice	2	4	3
Did not vote twice	11	15	16
	64	74	66
Switched between Con. and Lab.	5	3	5
Switched between major and minor parties	7	4	4
Switched between voting and non-voting	24	19	25
	36	26	34

Source: Crewe (1985a, p. 110).

less, it was this switching at the margins, together with the non-voting traffic, that accounted for short-term electoral change. 'Floating' of this kind appeared to be a response to rather vague short-term factors — the current images of the parties and how well governments handled the economy, for example — but, overall, floaters were less concerned and less knowledgeable about politics and less interested in the outcome of elections than were those whose voting pattern was stable. Paradoxically, it was not the politically interested and knowledgeable voters who determined which party won elections — since they were largely committed and loyal party supporters — but those whose concern with political affairs was peripheral (see Milne and MacKenzie, 1958, p. 192; Butler and Stokes, 1969, p. 437).

According to the model, longer-term electoral change would be very slow and gradual, depending upon demographic trends (the differential fertility and mortality of the different classes, for instance) and changes in the social structure and in patterns of socialisation. As we shall see in the next chapter, however, these expectations were not fulfilled in elections after 1970.

Notes

1. I use 'sex' rather than 'gender' because it is voting differences between the biologically defined sexes that is of interest here.

Gender differences — which relate to the roles assigned to males and females — are part of the explanation for political differences between the sexes.

2. I cannot give a precise reference for this suggestion but I once heard it on a Radio 4 programme about regional accents introduced by Brian Redhead.

3. There is a story of Keir Hardie, the founder of the Labour Party, haranguing a crowd of impoverished London dockers in the late nineteenth century about the merits of socialism. When he had finished he was asked, 'Yes, but what is your view on the disestablishment of the Church in Wales?'

4. Here and elsewhere the use of 'Northern England' or 'the North' refers to all three northern regions — the North, the North West and Yorkshire and Humberside.

3

PARTISAN AND CLASS DEALIGNMENT AFTER 1970

The British electorate of the 1950s and 1960s was portrayed as aligned in two important ways. There was a partisan alignment and a class alignment. Other social characteristics also aligned with party but more weakly than class. Not surprisingly, an electorate such as that described in Chapter 2 sustained a stable two-party system. The Conservative and Labour parties dominated elections and monopolised government; electoral change was slow and small.

Even the most casual observer must have noticed, however, that from the 1970s onwards the party system has been far from stable and electoral change has been swift and extensive. In general elections the two-party duopoly in England has been eroded, at first by the Liberals, then by the Liberals in alliance with the SDP and finally by the Liberal Democrats. At the same time, in Scotland and Wales the nationalist parties have become important and established features of the political landscape. During this period electoral volatility rather than stability has been conspicuous. There was even a period in the late 1970s when single-party government could not be sustained and a 'Lib-Lab' pact was required to keep the Labour government in office. Clearly something had gone wrong with the admittedly greatly simplified model of a stable, aligned electorate that I outlined in Chapter 2.

Having pictured the electorate as aligned, we can imagine that a process of *re*alignment could take place. Large sections of the electorate could stop identifying with one party and start to identify with another; some social group as a whole might switch its party allegiance. The most frequently cited example of a realignment like this is the case of black voters in the United States. Up to about 1928, when American blacks voted they usually supported the Republican party (on the perfectly reasonable grounds that President Abraham Lincoln, who freed the slaves, had been a Republican). From 1928 onwards, however, blacks began to switch to the Democratic party and today they are an overwhelmingly Democratic group.

There is no similar example of realignment in modern British political history. What largely explains the electoral turmoil of recent years, however, is a sort of half-way house between alignment and realignment, namely *dealignment*. This refers to a weakening of previously existing alignments. Partisan and class dealignment have been identified by numerous writers as the key processes underlying electoral behaviour during the last twenty-five years.

It is not, of course, that voters woke up on New Year's Day in 1970 and decided to start dealigning themselves. But 1970 does appear to be a convenient and sensible point from which to date a marked change in British electoral behaviour (see Franklin, 1985, ch. 7).[1]

Partisan dealignment

The first trend to be considered is partisan dealignment. In Chapter 2 (Table 2.1) we saw that most electors aligned themselves with parties in the sense of identifying with them.[2] Table 3.1 shows the trends in party identification after 1970.

The first row of the table shows that for most of this later period there has been a slight but perceptible decrease in the percentage of people volunteering a party identification. In 1992, however — possibly because there was a change in the order of the relevant questions in the 1992 BES survey — the percentage of identifiers was greater than ever recorded by the BES. Even excluding 1992, however, it is clear that most voters do still identify with parties.

Table 3.1 Trends in party identification (%).

	Average 1964–70	Feb. 1974	Oct. 1974	1979	1983	1987	1992
With party identification	90	88	88	85	86	86	94
With Conservative or Labour identification	81	75	74	74	67	67	78
'Very strong' identifiers	42	29	26	21	20	19	19
'Very strong' Conservative or Labour identifiers	40	27	23	19	18	16	18

Source: Figures to 1979 are from Sarlvik and Crewe (1983, pp. 334–6); those for 1983 to 1992 have been calculated directly from the relevant BES survey data.

Much more striking is the decline in the proportion whose commitment to their party is 'very strong', which is shown in the third row of the table. This did not recover in 1992 and the proportion has more than halved since the 1960s. In the late 1960s, more than two-fifths of the electorate thought of themselves as 'very strong' party supporters while by 1992 less than one-fifth did so. When it is remembered that stronger partisanship is associated with more stable voting, the implications of this weakening of partisan alignment are clear.

The second and fourth rows of Table 3.1 refer specifically to identification with the Labour and Conservative parties. In these cases the pattern of overall identification is repeated. In the 1960s just over 80 per cent of electors identified with the two major parties but by the 1980s this had fallen to two-thirds, only to rise again to 78 per cent in 1992. The percentage identifying 'very strongly' with either of the two parties has fallen steeply, however, from 40 per cent of the electorate before 1970 to only 16 per cent in 1987, and in 1992 it remained at the lower levels recorded after 1970.

On this evidence, then, people do still tend to align themselves psychologically with political parties, but they do so much less strongly than before and the predominance of the two major parties in this respect has been substantially reduced. This means that whereas the Conservatives and Labour both used to be able to rely on solid and consistent support from about 40 per cent of the voters, their core support is now much smaller.

Explaining partisan dealignment

What explains this weakening in the intensity of support for the parties? Why are people less strongly partisan? Answers to these questions are, of necessity, speculative to some extent. They also overlap with explanations for class dealignment which, for the sake of clarity of presentation, I have tried to keep separate and shall discuss later in this chapter. If we concentrate for the moment on the weakening of partisanship, there are four main lines of explanation that can be suggested.

1. *Increased political awareness: education.* As I noted in Chapter 2, one of the functions that identifying with a party served for the individual was to simplify the complex political world. Identification supplied 'cues' to the voter about how to evaluate policies, personalities and the actions of governments. Thus a very strong Conservative would believe, almost without thinking, that Conservative policies on taxation, health, the European Monetary System or anything else were 'good', and that Conservative leaders were 'best'; by definition the Labour party and all its works were 'bad'.

   If, however, voters have become more politically aware because they are better educated, they will have less need of such a psychological device to simplify the world. And it is certainly the case, in aggregate, that over the past thirty years the electorate has received more (though some might question whether it is better) education. The school-leaving age has been raised to 16; more pupils stay on at school beyond the minimum age (and more take A-level Politics); more students now enter higher education than ever before. It is possible that as the general educational level has risen, so has the level of political sophistication and, as a result, emotionally based attachments to political parties have declined in intensity.

   There is some supporting evidence at the individual level for this proposition. Crewe, Sarlvik and Alt (1977), in their seminal article on partisan dealignment, found that the decline in partisan strength up to 1974 was most marked among those who had gone on to higher education and least marked among those who left school at the minimum age (pp. 166–7). In addition, analysis of the 1992 BES data shows that only 14 per cent of respondents with a degree were 'very strong' party identifiers, compared with 25 per cent of those who left school when they were aged 15 or less. These data lend support to the argument that as the electorate has slowly become more highly educated, its dependence on the 'psychological crutch' afforded by party identification has decreased.

2. *Increased political awareness: television.* Increased political awareness and sophistication may also be a consequence of increased television coverage of politics. In the first place, it was not until the 1960s that ownership of television sets became well-nigh universal in Britain. Second, in its relatively short history the coverage of politics by television has changed both in extent and qualitatively.

It may be hard to believe nowadays, but during the 1955 general election campaign television news broadcasts made no references whatsoever to the election because the broadcasting authorities feared that if they covered the election, they would be in breach of the laws regulating the conduct of elections. It was only in the 1960s that campaign reports of the kind with which we are now familiar began to develop. Even outside campaign periods, television coverage of politics was initially limited and circumspect in the extreme. In the first half of the 1950s there was even a rule preventing discussion on television of matters that were about to be, or had recently been, debated in the House of Commons. When leading politicians deigned to be interviewed, they determined the questions to be asked and were treated in a highly deferential manner by interviewers.

The contrast with today could hardly be clearer. Intense and detailed coverage of politics is available for those who want to watch it. Television cameras give live coverage of debates in the House of Commons and MPs rush from the House to comment on debates still in progress for the benefit of the TV audience. Politicians of all parties are questioned aggressively and, indeed, if a party leader appears to have been given an 'easy ride' by an interviewer, complaints are loud and long. All of this may have increased the political knowledge and sophistication of the voters and thus, indirectly, weakened party commitment.

In subtle ways the style of political television also helps to diminish the strength of partisanship. News reporting tends to assume that the viewer has a dispassionate interest in hearing all sides of the story. Moreover, in political discussion programmes like the very popular *Question Time*, we all seem to be encouraged to be like the chairman, aloof from the party bickering. Partisans are projected as unreasonable ideologues and the viewer is encouraged to recognise that party representatives on the panel are putting forward a one-sided point of view. In addition, thirty years ago very few voters would ever have seen party leaders in the flesh and they could, therefore, quite easily idealise them or else think of them as 'hate' figures. Now we see them every week on the box, and it is manifest that they are neither gods nor devils. Labour politicians are not, on the whole, dripping blood as they prepare to pillage the savings of the thrifty, and most Conservatives do not come over as grim-faced capitalists bent on grinding down the poor.

Even entertainment shows serve to discourage voters from thinking that their party is something to be 'loved and trusted'.[3] Impressionists poke fun at politicians and the widely viewed satirical programme *Spitting Image* holds politicians of all parties up to ridicule in a savage way.[4]

It would be very difficult, if not impossible, to measure the effects of the messages transmitted to voters by the style of political television. By their nature they are diffuse and subtle. It would be surprising, however, if the clear decline in the strength of partisan commitment over the past twenty-five years were unrelated to the ways in which politics and politicians have been projected by television.

3. *The performance of the parties.* A more direct source of weakening party identification is the apparent lack of achievement that both major parties have had in office. Put minimally, neither has been a dazzling success. Governing a modern industrial society is a difficult and complex task, and no doubt voters are over-optimistic about what governments can achieve and too quick to blame governments when things go wrong. Nevertheless, the series of disappointments, policy failures and U-turns that have marked government performances, and the persistence of major problems facing the

Table 3.2   Approval of government record and satisfaction with the Prime Minister and Leader of the Opposition.

	Approval of government record	Satisfaction with	
		Prime Minister	Opposition Leader
1951–55	49	55	–
1955–59	43	52	43
1959–64	43	51	51
1964–66	45	58	41
1966–70	31	42	33
1970–74	33	37	49
1974–79	33	46	41
1979–83	33	39	32
1983–87	34	40	38
1987–92	34	39/51	36
1992–93 (Sept.)	19	31	45

Note: The figures are monthly averages of those saying that they 'approve' of the government's record to date, are 'satisfied' with the Prime Minister and think that the Leader of the Opposition is proving 'a good leader' of his or her party. For the period 1987–92 two figures are given for satisfaction with the Prime Minister: the first refers to Mrs Thatcher and the second to Mr Major.

Sources: *Gallup Political Index*, 1951–90; *Gallup Social, Political and Economic Index*, 1991–3.

country, must surely have shaken any conviction that voters might have had that 'their' party had all the answers.

Some evidence in support of this interpretation is given in Table 3.2, which shows that from 1966 onwards there was generally a markedly lower level of approval for the performances of governments, as compared with the period 1951–64. The Labour government of 1966–70 plumbed new depths of unpopularity but even in the 1970s and 1980s approval levels remained low.

Satisfaction with the performance of political leaders has also declined. Before 1966 more than half of the electorate, on average, was satisfied with the Prime Minister; after that the figure is closer to 40 per cent. The trend in ratings for Opposition leaders is less clear, but even so they are generally lower for the period after 1966 than before. It is perhaps unfair to include the period since the 1992 election in the table — the government and the Prime Minister can expect an upswing in approval ratings as we get closer to the next election. It is interesting to note, however, that their post-election ratings have declined more steeply than after any previous election.[5]

Much wider considerations than the performances of the parties may underlie these figures. Some commentators have argued that from the late 1960s, the electorate's expectations of government were unreasonably high; governments simply could not deliver what the voters expected and thus they were bound to be disappointed (see King, 1975). Others suggest that there has been a decline in deference among the electorate (partly sparked off by the music of the Beatles and the Rolling Stones). People have become less trustful of, and less willing to accept the authority of, government and political leaders (Beer, 1982). This relates to the argument about declining party identification, since identification itself implies a kind of deference to the authority of a political party.

4. *Ideological disjuncture.* A final source of weakening party identification refers specifically to the Labour party. Between 1964 and 1979 there was a significant decline in support for the basic ideological principles of the Labour party, even among Labour supporters, who were themselves declining in number. Crewe (1985a, p. 139) shows that among Labour identifiers the percentages favouring each aspect of Labour's 'collectivist trinity' of public ownership, trade union power and increased spending on social welfare, fell by more than twenty points between 1964 and 1979. By 1979, according to Crewe, there was an 'ideological chasm' between the Labour party and its supporters. Over an even longer period (1957–80), Martin Harrop (1982), using Gallup data, found a marked drop in the percentages of Labour voters who favoured restricting dividends and profits, cutting defence expenditure and abolishing the House of Lords.

Clearly, if there is an increasing disjuncture between the basic tenets of a party and the opinions of its supporters (let alone its potential supporters), we would expect commitment to the party on the part of its supporters to become more and more strained. Labour has recognised this problem and since the mid-1980s has embarked on a series of policy reviews designed to bring the party more in tune with the attitudes of voters (see Hughes and Wintour, 1990). This process is still ongoing but the danger for Labour is that in 'modernising' its appeal it will alienate committed members and supporters, who were attracted by the old ideology in the first place. A survey of Labour members carried out in 1989–90 found that 61 per cent thought that Labour should stick to its principles even if this should lose an election (Seyd and Whiteley, 1992, p. 134).

In summary, I have suggested that the progressive weakening of party identification which was shown in Table 3.1 is likely to have been a consequence of a combination of increased knowledge and sophistication about politics, the increased and changed nature of television coverage of politics, the relatively poor performances of the parties in office and the decline in support for collectivist values among Labour (and, presumably, even more so among former Labour) supporters.

Partisan dealignment has important consequences, which I shall consider more fully later in this chapter. Party identification was, however, just one of the pillars of electoral politics in the 1950s and 1960s. The other was class voting and it too has been crumbling.

Class dealignment

The relationship between class (defined according to manual or non-manual status) and party choice in elections since 1964 is shown in Table 3.3. There is a lot of information in this table which makes it somewhat difficult to interpret, but voting researchers have tried to devise summary measures of the relationship between class and vote which make comparisons over time easier.

There have been two widely used measures. The first can be calculated directly from the data in Table 3.3 and is called the 'Alford index' (since it was first used by a political scientist called Robert Alford). The index is calculated by simply subtracting Labour's percentage share of the vote among non-manual workers from its share among manual workers. Thus for 1964 the score is $(64 - 22) = 42$. A little thought will show that the index can vary between 0 (equal percentages vote Labour in each class and there is, therefore, no class voting) and 100 (all manual workers vote

Table 3.3   Occupational class and party choice, 1964–92 (%).

	1964		1966		1970	
	Non-manual	*Manual*	*Non-manual*	*Manual*	*Non-manual*	*Manual*
Conservative	62	28	60	25	64	33
Labour	22	64	26	69	25	58
Liberal	16	8	14	6	11	9

	Feb. 1974		Oct. 1974		1979	
	Non-manual	*Manual*	*Non-manual*	*Manual*	*Non-manual*	*Manual*
Conservative	53	24	51	24	60	35
Labour	22	57	25	57	23	50
Liberal	25	19	24	20	17	15

	1983		1987		1992	
	Non-manual	*Manual*	*Non-manual*	*Manual*	*Non-manual*	*Manual*
Conservative	55	35	54	35	56	36
Labour	17	42	20	45	24	51
Liberal, etc.	28	22	27	21	21	14

Note: 'Liberal, etc.' in the last row refers to the Liberal-SDP Alliance in 1983 and 1987 and to the Liberal Democrats in 1992.

Sources: Figures from 1964 to 1983 are from Heath *et al.* (1985, p. 30); 1987 and 1992 data are calculated from the relevant BES data.

Labour, no non-manual workers do). By convention, it is Labour voting that is used as the basis for calculating the Alford index but Conservative voting could just as easily be used.[6] The index is, then, a measure of the relative strength of a party in two classes. It is a measure of 'relative class voting'.

A second measure of class voting is the percentage of voters who support their 'natural' class party. In other words, it is the number of non-manual workers voting Conservative plus the number of manual workers voting Labour, as a percentage of all voters. This is called 'absolute class voting'. This measure cannot be derived directly from the data in Table 3.3 since to calculate it we need to know the *numbers* rather than the percentages in each cell.

Table 3.4 shows the Alford index scores for both parties and the level of absolute class voting in elections since 1964. Despite the fact that class voting appears to have increased slightly in 1992, all

Table 3.4   Measures of class voting, 1964–92.

	1964	1966	1970	Feb. 1974	Oct. 1974	1979	1983	1987	1992
Alford index (Labour)	42	43	33	35	32	27	25	25	27
Alford index (Conservative)	34	35	31	29	27	25	20	19	20
Absolute class voting	63	66	60	55	54	55	47	49	54

Source: Alford index scores are calculated from the data given in Table 3.3. Absolute class voting figures for 1964–83 are from Heath *et al.* (1985, p. 30); 1987 and 1992 figures are calculated from the relevant BES data.

three measures indicate that the relationship between class and vote has been less strong since the 1970s than it was before. The Alford index scores indicate that class voting still exists (scores remain greater than 0) but its level in the 1980s and 1990s has been considerably lower than it was in the 1960s. Similarly, whereas around two-thirds of voters used to support their 'natural' class party, this is now true of about half of the voters for the three main parties.[7]

This is the basic evidence for the argument that the period after 1970 witnessed a clear weakening of the alignment between class and party — a class dealignment — among the British electorate. The same conclusion is reached by authors who have undertaken more complicated statistical analyses (see Franklin, 1985, ch. 4; Rose and McAllister, 1986, ch. 3; 1990, ch. 4).

Explaining class dealignment

Why has there been this weakening of the alignment between class and party choice? Explanations are, as I have indicated, very much bound up with explanations of partisan dealignment. As Crewe puts it, 'it is easier to vote against one's class once party loyalties weaken, easier to abandon one's party once class loyalties wither' (1984, p. 193). Clearly the points that I made in trying to explain partisan dealignment are also relevant here. There are, however, a number of additional causes to which one might point. It would be naive, of course, to expect that a phenomenon as complex as class dealignment would have one simple cause. Rather, it is a product of a series of interlocking developments.

1. *Embourgeoisement (again).* In Chapter 2 I briefly discussed the testing and rejection of the 'embourgeoisement thesis' — the view that the working class were becoming more bourgeois and hence Conservative — in the early 1960s. The kinds of developments that led people to speculate about the possibility of embourgeoisement at that time have continued apace. Despite the persistence of pockets of poverty and the growth of a poor 'underclass' during the 1980s, manual workers on the whole have become even more affluent. More and more own their own homes and consumer durables like cars, telephones and so on; some have become shareholders. At least on the surface, differences between, say, skilled manual workers and lower non-manual groups — or even traditionally solid middle-class groups like schoolteachers — are not all that obvious. If, as Goldthorpe and Lockwood found, support for the Labour party among more affluent workers is more conditional and less 'solidaristic' than it was among traditional workers, and we ally this to the voters' dim view of the performance of the parties in office, then it seems likely that the spread of affluence among the working class has created at least the potential for reduced working-class Labour voting.

2. *Changes in the occupational and industrial structures.* The last thirty years have seen very fundamental changes in the occupational and industrial structure of Britain. Three features especially deserve to be noted. First, there has been a shift from manual to non-manual work. In 1961 manual workers comprised 58 per cent of the workforce; by 1981 this had fallen to 45 per cent (Heath and McDonald, 1987). For the first time since records began, manual workers became a minority of the workforce. To some extent the growth in non-manual employment has been associated with inter-generational upward social mobility. Many people from working-class backgrounds now have professional and other non-manual occupations, and this has diluted the previously solid Conservative allegiance of the middle class.

Second, there has been a shift from employment in manufacturing to the service sector. In 1961, 38 per cent of employees worked in manufacturing and 47 per cent in services. By 1991 manufacturing was down to 22 per cent and the service sector up to 71 per cent (Central Statistical Office, 1993). Put simply, there are fewer coal miners around today and more hairdressers.

Third, even within manufacturing there has been an especially sharp contraction in heavy industries like coal mining, steel, shipbuilding and textiles. These are traditionally highly unionised industries with large plants, which tended to create distinctive and homogeneous working-class communities. In contrast, the emerging 'sunrise' industries are less heavily unionised and rarely located at the centre of established working-class communities.

Taken together, it seems likely that these sorts of changes have undermined the general level of class consciousness and class solidarity which underpinned the class–party relationship.

3. *Cross-class locations.* Partly as a consequence of these developments, and partly as a result of the increased proportion of women in the workforce, more and more people are in 'cross-class' locations. That is, they either individually have characteristics of more than one class or else live in mixed-class households. Thus, in the mid-1950s only about 20 per cent of manual workers were home-owners, whereas the figure is now well over half. On the other hand, trade union membership (traditionally a characteristic of manual workers) has increased sharply among white-collar employees. Rose (1980, p. 29) found that in 1979 only 14 per cent of the electorate conformed to a stereotype of either the middle or the working class compared with 23 per cent in 1970.

The growth of female employment (especially in non-manual jobs) has contributed to an increase in mixed-class families. By the 1970s over a third of the growing number of households in which both husband and wife had jobs were 'mixed class' in the sense that one partner had a non-manual job while the other was a manual worker. When the effects of intergenerational mobility are added to this, the result is that more than half of all extended families — grandparents, parents and children — are mixed in their class composition. Again this reduces the potential for class solidarity in electoral behaviour.

4. *Sectoral cleavages.* According to Patrick Dunleavy (1980), party choice after 1970 was still basically a product of social location. What happened, however, was that the old cleavage based on occupational class was replaced by two new cleavages. The first relates to sector of employment — whether it is the public or the private sector — and its importance is a consequence of the sharp growth in public-sector employment in Britain (at least up to the 1980s). In 1961, 24 per cent of all employees worked for the state; by 1982 the figure was 31 per cent (Dunleavy and Husbands, 1985, p. 21). The second cleavage relates to sector of consumption. People who live in council houses, use public transport and depend on the NHS for medical treatment need these services to be collectively provided. They are consumers in the public sector. In contrast, people who own their own homes, use cars rather than buses or trains and have their own medical insurance arrangements are consumers in the private sector. The groups created by these production and consumption cleavages are in different social locations and they have conflicting interests which are translated, according to Dunleavy, into differential voting behaviour. Those in the private sectors favour the Conservatives; those in the public sectors do not.

Dunleavy's theory is not without its critics (see, especially, Franklin, 1985, ch. 2), and supporting evidence is stronger on the consumption than on the production side. None the less, the sectoral cleavage approach helps to account for the growth in non-Conservative support among white-collar employees in the public sector (such as teachers and social workers) and it provides a solid theoretical basis for the increased importance of housing tenure as a predictor of party choice.

5. *Fragmented working-class interests.* Ivor Crewe does not subscribe entirely to the sectoral cleavage thesis, but has a somewhat similar argument. Crewe (1981a, 1985b, 1992a, 1992b) suggests that part of the explanation for class dealignment is the increased fragmentation of class (especially working-class)

interests. Manual workers who are owner-occupiers or who work in the private sector have different interests from those who are council tenants or who are public sector workers. As the tax net has widened, even moderately well-off workers have different interests (lower taxes) from the poor (higher taxes, increased welfare benefits). Workers living in the affluent and expanding South East are likely to want economic and industrial policies that are different from those favoured by people living in the North and Scotland. Workers who belong to powerful trade unions benefit from free, collective pay bargaining; those in weak unions or in none do not.

Crewe uses these sorts of differences to distinguish a 'traditional' working class (manual workers who live in Scotland and the North, are council tenants, union members and public-sector employees) and a 'new' working class (manual workers who live in the South, are owner-occupiers, not union members and are private-sector employees). The 'new' working class is increasingly dominant within the working class as a whole and its support for Labour is very weak.

6. *Labour party success.* All the preceding explanations of the decline in class voting emphasise social change. A rather different point of view is offered by Mark Franklin (1985), whose explanation is more directly political. He argues that, paradoxically, it was the very success of the Labour government of 1945–51 that laid the basis for future problems. The Attlee government achieved Labour's 'historic mission' of eliminating grinding poverty and establishing a modern welfare state. Thereafter Labour had no sense of direction. It was no longer part of a crusade to change society but merely one among a number of parties seeking office. As such, it came to be judged like any other party on its competence and policies. While Labour's policies may have continued to attract middle-class socialists, their appeal to working-class voters declined.

As I suggested above, none of these explanations by themselves account for class dealignment. There is no single explanation. Rather, a variety of social changes and political developments have come together and interacted to produce a weakening of the class alignment.

The debate over class dealignment

The argument that the British electorate was undergoing a process of dealignment after 1970 can be fairly described as the orthodoxy in British electoral studies up to the mid-1980s. This view was held by the leading academic specialists and was accepted by many political commentators and practising politicians. In 1985, however, Anthony Heath, Roger Jowell and John Curtice published their book *How Britain Votes*, reporting the results of the British Election Study survey of the 1983 general election, in which they directly challenged the prevailing orthodoxy. Their conclusion, that there had been no class dealignment, provoked furious debate.

How Britain Votes: a revisionist view

The argument and analysis concerning class dealignment put forward by Heath, Jowell and Curtice can be summarised in five stages.

1. *Redefinition of class.* Heath *et al.* rejected the traditional manual/non-manual dichotomy as 'wholly inadequate for studying the social bases of politics'. They also rejected the market research social grading schemes (A, B, C1, etc.). Their own categorisation is based on economic interests and divides the electorate into five categories as follows:

   (a) The salariat: managers, administrators, supervisors, professionals and semi-professionals.
   (b) Routine non-manual: clerks, salesworkers, secretaries ('a kind of white-collar labour force').
   (c) The petty bourgeoisie: farmers, small proprietors and own-account manual workers.
   (d) Foremen and technicians: ('a kind of blue-collar élite').
   (e) The working class: 'rank and file manual employees'.

   Perhaps the most striking difference between this and more common classifications is the way in which it spreads manual workers across three different groups — (c), (d) and (e). Thus, a self-employed plumber would be in group (c), a foreman plumber in group (d) and a plumber employed by a company in group (e). More traditional categorisations would classify all plumbers as skilled manual workers.

2. *Rejection of absolute class voting.* The percentage of the electorate who support their 'natural' class party (the measure of absolute class voting) is not, claimed Heath *et al.*, a useful way of either thinking about or measuring the level of class voting. They said that this was not what commentators had in mind when they talked about the declining class basis of voting, and as a measure it is misleading, since it is affected by the level of support that the parties obtain at particular elections. If Labour is doing badly overall, this is likely to mean that a smaller proportion of working-class people is voting Labour and in turn this will produce a decline in absolute class voting. Rather, they asserted, what commentators had in mind was an increase in 'cross-class' voting — manual workers voting Conservative and non-manual workers voting Labour — that is, changes in the *relative* support for the parties in the different classes. What should be measured is relative, not absolute, class voting.

3. *Measuring relative class voting.* Heath and his colleagues also rejected the Alford index as a measure of class voting, preferring instead the 'odds ratio'. This is the odds of a person in the middle class voting Conservative rather than Labour, divided by the corresponding odds for a working-class person. Thus, using the data in Table 3.3, the odds of a non-manual worker voting Conservative rather than Labour in 1964 were 62:22 whereas for a manual worker they were 28:64. The odds ratio is, therefore, $(62/22)/(28/64) = 6.4$. The larger the odds ratio, the stronger is relative class voting.

4. *No class dealignment.* Using their new class categories, Heath *et al.* calculated odds ratios for the salariat and the working class. The scores for elections between 1964 and 1983 are as follows:

1964	9.3	1966	7.3	1970	3.9	Feb. 1974	6.1
Oct. 1974	6.4	1979	4.9	1983	6.3		

They argued that these figures do not suggest a steady decline but rather a 'trendless fluctuation' and that there had been, therefore, no progressive class dealignment.

5. *Explaining Labour's decline*. Proponents of the dealignment thesis used the idea of dealignment to explain the changing fortunes of the parties and, in particular, the electoral decline of the Labour party. Since Heath and his colleagues denied that there had been a dealignment, they looked elsewhere to account for Labour's lack of success in the 1980s. They suggested that changes in the relative sizes of the different classes had been more important than any change in the level of class voting. Between 1964 and 1983 the working class contracted while the salariat and routine non-manual classes expanded, and this alone accounted for nearly half of Labour's decline in support between these two elections.

The argument put forward by Heath, Jowell and Curtice in *How Britain Votes* is complicated and in places difficult to follow, although I have simplified it somewhat here. Clearly, however, their work represented a major challenge to the orthodox view about the changing relationship between class and party choice, and it was a challenge that did not go unanswered. *How Britain Votes* was subjected to some very vigorous criticism (see especially Crewe, 1986, and Dunleavy, 1987). The debate prompted by the book (see Heath *et al.*, 1987) became rather technical (as well as tetchy) but there were four main areas of criticism.

First, although the new class schema proposed and used in *How Britain Votes* was not in itself greatly criticised, it is worth noting that it has the effect of 'minoritising' the working class. Between 1964 and 1983 the working class, as defined by Heath *et al.*, declined from 47 per cent to 34 per cent of the electorate, leaving it not much larger than the salariat which increased from 18 per cent to 27 per cent in the same period (Heath *et al.*, 1985, p. 36). In the words of Rose and McAllister, 'In effect, the working class is made into a residual minority, a virtual lumpenproletariat of manual workers lacking authority, autonomy, job security and social esteem' (1986, p. 45). It does seem strange to use the term 'working class' to describe only one-third of the electorate, especially given that on their own figures 60 per cent of the 1983 electorate thought of themselves as working class (Heath *et al.*, 1987, p. 274).

There is another more technical point to be made here. In order to analyse the relationship between class and vote over time, Heath and his colleagues had to recode the occupations of all respondents to all the election surveys since 1964. They did this by computer and it seems a remarkable piece of luck that the original codings, designed with a different class scheme in mind, could all be transformed to a unique category under the new scheme, without error or even a bit of fudging at the edges. Indeed, examination of the proportion of voters coded into each of the new classes at each election suggested to Dunleavy (1987, p. 409) that 'coding consistency across the years is rather problematic'. Taken together with the sensitivity of the odds ratio (see below), this raises doubts about the trend (or lack of trend) in class voting alleged by Heath and his colleagues.

Second, the section in *How Britain Votes* in which the level of absolute class voting is rejected as an appropriate test of dealignment is particularly compressed and difficult to understand. If, however, by dealignment we mean something like 'a decline in the propensity of middle-class people to vote Conservative and working-class people to vote Labour', it is plain that a fall in the proportion of the electorate voting for their 'natural' class party *is* some sort of indicator of dealignment. If fewer people are voting for their class party (which Heath *et al.* do not deny), then the relationship between class and party is surely weakening. Moreover, Crewe (1986) effectively rebuts Heath *et al.*'s technical objection to using absolute class voting as a measure (that it is heavily affected by Labour's electoral fortunes) by showing that this in fact makes only a tiny difference to the scores obtained.

Third, the most ferocious criticisms of Heath *et al.*'s analysis related to their use of odds ratios to measure class voting. Dunleavy (1987) describes the measure as, among other things, 'quite inappropriate', 'distorting', 'peculiar', 'eccentric' and 'virtually meaningless'.

The first problem with the odds ratio is that it is highly sensitive to very small changes in the percentages used as the basis for calculation. On the basis of their sample, Heath and his colleagues estimate the ratio of Conservative to Labour voting among the salariat in 1983 as 54:14. If it had actually been 50:18, which is not greatly different, the resulting odds ratio for 1983 would be 4.5 instead of 6.3 and this might suggest a clear downward trend. The sensitivity of odds ratios is particularly important given my comments above on the problems of coding occupations and the question of sampling error mentioned in Chapter 1. Crewe argues that the odds ratio 'offers a spurious degree of precision and converts tiny ripples of movement — whether real or illusory — into dramatic tides of change' (1986, p. 626).

A second criticism of the odds ratios presented by Heath *et al.* is that the calculation of Conservative/Labour odds ignores support for other parties. If it were found that 4 per cent of the working class voted Labour and 1 per cent Conservative, and that 4 per cent of the middle class voted Conservative and 1 per cent Labour (with everyone else voting Liberal Democrat), then that would produce the same odds ratio (16.0) as would be produced by a situation in which the respective figures were 80 per cent and 20 per cent with no one voting Liberal Democrat. To argue that the two situations exhibit the same level of class voting seems perverse.

The odds ratios presented in *How Britain Votes*, moreover, relate only to party choice among the salariat and the working class. By 1983 these two classes accounted for only three-fifths of the electorate and, in addition, on Heath *et al.*'s figures it is only between these two of the five classes that there has been no steady convergence in party choice. If class dealignment were taking place we would not expect to find it most pronounced among the core components of the middle and working classes. Rather, we would expect dealignment to occur more noticeably among more peripheral groups such as routine non-manual workers or skilled manual workers.

The fourth area of criticism concerns Heath *et al.*'s claim that the impact of changes in the sizes of the different classes upon the electoral performance of the parties 'has probably been far greater' than changes in the behaviour of people within the classes (p. 36). No one would deny that such structural change is important, but their own calculations show that it explains less than half of Labour's decline between 1964 and 1983 and hardly anything of the rise in third-party support. Furthermore, it should have meant a rise of 5.5 points in Conservative support whereas this actually fell by one point. This is not very convincing. In addition, Crewe (1986) demonstrates that changes in voting patterns within classes between 1964 and 1983 account for changes in the levels of support for the parties more accurately than do changes in the class structure.

Taken together, these are a powerful set of criticisms. Undeterred, however, Heath, Jowell and Curtice returned to the fray in their report on the 1987 election (Heath *et al.*, 1991).

Understanding Political Change: the debate continued

Figures for class voting in the 1983, 1987 and 1992 elections, using the classes defined by Heath *et al.*, are given in Table 3.5. On these data the salariat/working-class odds ratio was 6.9 in 1983, 5.8 in 1987 and 4.9 in 1992, which implies declining class voting. In *Understanding Political Change*, however, Heath *et al.* abandon the use of odds ratios to measure class voting and use instead log-linear analysis, a technique that enables the strength of the relationship between class and party choice to be assessed while controlling for, or taking account of, changes in the sizes of the different classes and changes in the overall shares of the vote gained by the different parties.[8] On this basis, the hypothesis that relative class voting was equally strong at all elections from 1964 to 1987 is well supported but not fully confirmed. Heath *et al.* therefore modify their previous position slightly and concede that there was indeed a sharp decline in class voting between 1964 and 1970. They maintain, however, that after 1970 there was no steady downward trend but 'trendless fluctuations' (at least up to 1987) in the level of class voting. In explaining the variations in class voting since 1964, Heath *et al.* emphasise political factors — such as the disappointing performances of Labour governments and the sharp increase in the number of constituencies contested by 'centre' party candidates — rather than any weakening of class divisions or loosening of the social structure.

Compared with the storm which greeted Heath *et al.*'s attack on the class dealignment thesis in *How Britain Votes*, the reception accorded to this aspect of *Understanding Political Change* has been relatively muted (see, however, Crewe, 1992c). In large part this is because critics have concluded that what is at issue between them and Heath *et al.* is simply a matter of definition, or 'semantics rather than substance' as Miller, Clarke, Harrop, Leduc and Whiteley put it (1990, p. 8). Class dealignment, as generally understood, focuses on absolute as well as relative class voting while Heath *et al.* persist in asserting that the absolute propensity of members of a class to

Table 3.5 Class and party choice, 1983–92, using Heath et al.'s class scheme (%).

	Salariat	Routine non-manual	Petty bourgeoisie	Foremen/ technicians	Working class
1983					
Conservative	55	53	71	44	30
Labour	13	20	12	28	49
Alliance	31	27	17	28	21
	(793)	(547)	(227)	(183)	(1,127)
1987					
Conservative	56	52	65	39	31
Labour	15	26	16	36	48
Alliance	29	23	20	24	21
	(839)	(576)	(245)	(176)	(1,024)
1992					
Conservative	56	53	66	41	32
Labour	20	30	17	45	56
Alliance	25	17	18	15	12
	(651)	(560)	(163)	(116)	(783)

Note: The figures shown in brackets are the numbers on which the percentages are based.
Sources: 1983 and 1987 figures are from Heath *et al.* (1991), p. 69; 1992 data are taken directly from the BES 1992 cross-section survey.

vote for a particular party is not what is meant by class voting. While their analysis in *Understanding Political Change* is a valuable correction to a view that *relative* class voting has declined in a steady, step-by-step way, the fact remains that smaller proportions of middle-class people vote Conservative and smaller proportions of working-class people vote Labour than used to be the case. In other words, the alignment between class and party is less strong than it was — there has been a dealignment.

The consequences of dealignment: electoral volatility

Together, the processes of class and partisan dealignment are the most striking developments in British electoral behaviour during the last thirty years. In particular, the decline in the average strength of party identification among electors — about which there is no dispute — seems likely to have had important consequences. Strong party identification acts as a sort of psychological anchor in the sea of electoral politics. It provides an element of stability, and for very strong identifiers party choice at elections is nearly automatic. When the anchor is removed, or more weakly attached, voters are likely to be more open to persuasion, more indecisive about which party to vote for, and more likely to switch parties. The core of support upon which each party can rely is much diminished in size. The party system, rather than being set in stone, as it were, is more unstable; its foundations are less solid and secure. In short, dealignment is likely to produce an electorate that is very different from that described by voting studies in the 1950s and 1960s. Rather than being stable and predictable as far as party choice is concerned, voters are likely to be volatile and unpredictable in their behaviour.

Defining electoral volatility is not straightforward, however. First of all we have to distinguish *net* and *overall* volatility. The distinction is similar to that between swing and the 'flow of the vote' between elections (see Chapter 1). Net volatility usually refers to the change in the parties' shares of the votes at two successive elections (although it could also apply to the share of voting intentions received in successive opinion polls), while overall volatility refers to the total amount of changing that takes place in order to produce the net outcome. Thus, self-cancelling changes — some people switch from Conservative to Labour while others switch from Labour to the Conservatives — are part of overall volatility but would not affect net volatility. Indeed, it would be perfectly possible to imagine a situation in which there was no net volatility at all while overall volatility was high. I consider trends in net volatility in Chapter 6, but here the focus is on overall or individual volatility.

What, then, do we mean precisely by overall volatility? As indicated in the previous paragraph, the simplest understanding relates to voter behaviour in successive elections — 'inter-election' volatility. Those who behave differently, whether by switching parties or by moving between voting and non-voting, are volatile. But there are two further ways in which volatility can be understood.

The first might be termed 'mid-term movements'. Between general elections almost all voters have the opportunity to vote in local elections and some vote in by-elections. Monthly opinion polls give estimates of how the electorate would vote if there were a general election 'tomorrow'. A cursory glance at these indicators of mid-term party support shows that they fluctuate wildly as compared with the previous general election, so that we have here another dimension of electoral volatility.

The second additional dimension can be called 'campaign swithering', to borrow a useful Scots word used by William Miller in this context. During a general election campaign there are almost daily opinion polls and some panel surveys. These show that while some voters have their minds made up about which party to support when the campaign begins and never waver from that position, others are slow to decide, hesitant, or actually switch between parties — they are 'swithering'. This is another form of volatility.

In order to measure overall volatility in its different dimensions survey data are required and, ideally, it should be data from a panel survey or series of surveys that is used, since this minimises the risk of respondents misremembering how they voted in a previous election. Figures for levels of inter-election volatility from the series of BES surveys are given in Table 3.6. The first row of the table shows the percentages of those who voted who switched parties in successive elections (ignoring those that were separated by an unusually short time). The second row includes non-voters at either of the elections concerned and counts moving between voting and non-voting as volatile.

Not unexpectedly, when non-voting is included in the calculation volatility estimates are higher than when only party switching is considered. Indeed, more detailed figures show that switching between the Conservative and Labour parties is always the least

Table 3.6 Trends in electoral volatility (%).

	1959–64	1966–70*	1970–74 (Feb.)*	1974 (Oct.)–79*	1979–83	1983–87*	1987–92*
Switched parties	18	16	24	22	23	19	19
Switched (inc. non-voters)	35	34	42	37	40	37	34

Note: For pairs of elections marked with an asterisk, the data are derived partly or entirely from panel surveys.

Sources: Heath *et al.* (1991, p. 20) and 1987–92 BES panel survey.

common form of inter-election volatility. Switching between major and minor parties is more frequent, while moving between voting and non-voting is usually the most common form of individual change between elections.

What is striking about the figures in Table 3.6, however, as Heath *et al.* point out, is the apparent lack of any consistent long-term trend in either measure. Contrary to expectations, there is no clear upward trend in volatility. Rather, it seems that inter-election volatility increased a good deal in the 1970s and early 1980s but then reduced again to levels comparable with those found in the 1960s.

The evidence of monthly opinion polls and parliamentary by-elections suggests that mid-term movements in party support became much more violent from the late 1960s onwards and that this form of volatility has remained at a high level (see Crewe, 1985a, pp. 104–5; Norris, 1990). This is evidence about net volatility, however, and for overall volatility we have to consider panel surveys involving a mid-term wave.

As part of a 1983–87 panel, Heath *et al.* themselves also interviewed their sample in 1986. They found that, whereas 71 per cent of these respondents voted the same way in both 1983 and 1987, only 61 per cent supported the same party on all three occasions (Heath *et al.*, 1991, p. 29). Similarly, using up to five interviews at different points between 1983 and 1987 and considering only support for the three major British parties, Miller *et al.* (1990, p. 33) estimate that only 55 per cent of voters maintained consistent support for one party during the early and mid-1980s. For strong party identifiers the figure was 71 per cent, for medium strong identifiers 49 per cent, and for weak identifiers only 29 per cent. Although they have no comparable data for earlier periods, Miller *et al.* are in no doubt that by the 1980s the British electorate was characterised by high volatility in the periods between elections.

'Campaign swithering' takes two main forms — switching parties or moving between indecision and a firm voting intention ('churning', as the pollsters describe it). Campaign panel studies to measure this form of volatility are relatively recent and rare but the BES research on the 1992 election involved interviewing a panel of voters (by telephone) during and immediately after the campaign. Comparing respondents' campaign voting intention with their reported vote after the election, shows that while only

Table 3.7   'Late deciders' and 'waverers' 1964–92 (%).

| | | | | Feb. | Oct. | | | | |
	1964	*1966*	*1970*	*1974*	*1974*	*1979*	*1983*	*1987*	*1992*
Decided during campaign	12	11	12	23	22	28	22	21	24
Thought of voting for other party	25	23	21	25	21	31	25	28	26

Source: Heath *et al.* (1991, p. 15) and BES 1992 cross-section survey.

about 3 per cent of voters switched from a firm voting intention to a different party, 22 per cent had not made up their minds when first interviewed but did vote for one of the parties in the election.[9] A more exhaustive panel study at the time of the 1987 election, which involved four separate interviews, led Miller *et al.* to conclude that 'a huge 38 per cent of the electorate changed their party preferences one or more times in the short period between March 1987 and the election in June' (1990, p. 234).

Although 1992 was the first election at which the BES used a campaign panel, the main BES surveys provide a valuable series of data going back to 1964 which measures what Heath *et al.* call 'hesitancy' during campaigns — the percentage of voters who decided which party to support during the election campaign itself, and the percentage who thought of voting for a party other than the one for which they ended up voting. The figures are shown in Table 3.7. There were clearly more late deciders from 1974 onwards and the average percentage of waverers in the later period is higher than before, but Heath *et al.* point out that in February 1974 there were changes in the questions used to elicit this information and decline to commit themselves on any comparison between the two periods. The changes in question wording appear to me to be relatively trivial and it is at least arguable that the higher rates of 'hesitancy' found after 1970 are not artefacts of changed question wording but reflect genuine change among the electorate.[10]

The evidence for increased electoral volatility is, then, far from clear-cut. There does not appear to be a clear, long-term trend in inter-election volatility matching the trend in strength of party identification. On the other hand, if volatility is defined more widely, it does seem to be the case that the electorate is more unstable than it used to be. The potential for electoral change is greater. The analysis of the various dimensions of volatility is handicapped by the absence of suitable data from the pre-dealignment period, but there is general agreement among analysts that the modern electorate is unpredictable and volatile and, with the exception of Heath *et al.*, most believe that the level of unpredictability and volatility is greater than it was in the era of alignment.

Other social characteristics

If the influence of occupational class upon party choice has declined, what of the other social factors discussed in Chapter 2?

As far as age is concerned, the relationship with party choice also seems to have weakened. The figures in Table 3.8 show that in two out of the last three elections the youngest age group has given a plurality of votes to the Conservatives and in no case did Labour's share approach 50 per cent. The stereotype of radicalism in youth no longer seems to apply (unless radicalism is no longer associated with Labour voting). Perhaps young people no longer have 'heart'. Moreover, while Conservative support still tends to

Table 3.8 Party choice by age, 1983–87 (%).

	Under 25	*25–44*	*45–64*	*65+*
1983				
Conservative	43	44	44	52
Labour	32	27	30	28
Alliance	23	28	25	19
1987				
Conservative	36	41	47	50
Labour	41	32	29	27
Alliance	22	26	22	23
1992				
Conservative	41	43	48	49
Labour	37	34	33	36
Liberal Democrat	18	19	16	14

Note: Columns do not total 100 because figures for 'others' are not shown.

Sources: Figures for 1983 and 1987 are calculated from table 1.3 in Crewe, Day and Fox (1991); the 1992 figures are from the BES cross-section survey.

Table 3.9   The gender gap in British elections, 1964–92.

1964	1966	1970	Feb. 1974	Oct. 1974	1979	1983	1987	1992
4	8	11	3	8	3	2	1	6

Note: The scores given are women (% Con. – % Lab.) minus men (% Con. – % Lab.). A positive figure indicates that women are more Conservative than men and this is the case for every election.
Source: Norris (1993).

increase and Labour's to decline with age, the changes are not as regular or as sharp as was the case in the 1960s.

Similarly, the 'gender gap' all but disappeared in the 1980s, although it did re-emerge to some extent in 1992. Table 3.9 shows the Conservative lead over Labour among women minus the Conservative lead over Labour among men. Thus a positive score means that the Conservatives did better among women than among men. By 1987 there was hardly any difference between the sexes. In 1992, according to Pippa Norris (1993), there was a 'gender-generation' gap in that, among voters aged less than 30, the gender gap score was –14 (women less Conservative than men), while for those aged 30–65 it was +8, and for the over 65s it was +18. When structural factors such as class are taken into account, however, sex is not significantly related to party choice among younger voters. This is not the case with older voters and the Conservative advantage among older women remains difficult to explain.

I suggested in Chapter 2 that when Butler and Stokes examined British voting behaviour, the effect of religion upon party choice was already on the wane. Since then, religious adherence and practice have declined further in Britain. Although religion remains an important determinant of party choice in some other countries, it is now rarely given detailed consideration in major works on British electoral behaviour. The BES survey of the February 1974 election did not even ask respondents their religion and there is no entry for religion in the index of *How Britain Votes*.

None the less, Rose and McAllister (1986, pp. 72–4; 1990, pp. 48–50) reported that in the 1980s there remained a tendency for Anglicans to be more favourably disposed to the Conservatives than members of other denominations and people of no religion,

Table 3.10   Labour lead over Conservatives among working-class voters, 1964 and 1987.

	1964	1987
Wales	+64	+55
Scotland	+65	+52
North	+42	+35
Midlands	+44	+2
South	+31	−14

Source: Calculated from Heath *et al.* (1991), tables 7.6 and 7.7.

and in their report on the 1987 election Heath *et al.* 'rediscovered' religion. They found, somewhat to their surprise, that among the salariat there had been hardly any weakening of the association between religious affiliation and party choice since 1964.[11] Particularly noteworthy in 1987 was the high level of support for the Alliance among middle-class Nonconformists (42 per cent).

The fourth social influence discussed in Chapter 2 — region and locality — has increased in importance since the 1960s. The clearest evidence of this is in election results (see Chapter 6) but evidence at the individual level is given in Table 3.10. This shows Labour's lead over the Conservatives, among working-class voters only, in five regions. There clearly were already regional differences in 1964 but by 1987 Labour was actually behind among its 'natural' supporters in the South and only just obtained more working-class votes in the Midlands while maintaining large leads in the other regions. These differences persist even when allowance is made for the housing tenure, trade union membership and other social characteristics of the survey respondents.

While the influence of some social variables has waned, others have become more important. One of these is housing tenure. In earlier voting studies, tenure was generally considered to be an aspect of class but it now appears to have a strong independent effect upon party choice. According to Rose and McAllister (1986, p. 92; 1990, p. 87), tenure was the best single social predictor of party from the election of October 1974 to 1987.

Table 3.11 shows the clear effect of housing tenure within two of the class categories used by Heath and his colleagues. Almost all households in Britain are either owner-occupiers (or are buying their house) or council tenants. Fewer than 10 per cent have other

Table 3.11   Conservative lead over Labour by class and housing tenure, 1983–92.

	Intermediate classes		Working class	
	Owner-occupiers	Council tenants	Owner-occupiers	Council tenants
1983	+45	–25	+2	–42
1987	+39	–37	–2	–41
1992	+35	–42	–5	–52

Note: Figures for voters in the 'salariat' are not given since very few of them are council tenants.

Source: Heath *et al.* (1985, p. 46); 1987 and 1992 BES cross-section surveys.

forms of tenure. The sharp differences between the two groups have been explained in two main ways. First, they have different or even conflicting interests. Owner-occupiers benefit from tax relief on mortgage repayments and have an interest in low mortgage rates and low local taxes. Subsidising public housing or even simply building council housing can be seen as a 'cost' to them. Council tenants, on the other hand, do not benefit from mortgage tax relief and have an interest in keeping council rents rather than taxes low. In addition, housing is very much a politicised issue, with the Labour and Conservative parties being clearly identified with different policies.

The second explanation concentrates on socialisation processes and the neighbourhood effect mentioned in Chapter 2. People with the same housing tenure usually live in close physical proximity. There is a kind of residential segregation between council estates, modern private estates and areas of well established substantial houses. This creates local communities in which residents interact constantly, and this reinforces the dominant political values of the community.

A second social characteristic which has become more important electorally is race. Little attention was paid to the voting patterns of ethnic minorities in Britain in the 1950s and 1960s, largely because there were relatively few voters of Afro-Caribbean or Asian origin. Any national sample would have contained only a handful of such voters. As their numbers have increased, however (in particular the number of British-born ethnic minority voters), they have increased in political importance. This is highlighted by the fact that the ethnic minority population is concentrated in areas such as London, Leicester, Birmingham, Bradford and parts of the North West. As a consequence, many individual constituencies have a large ethnic minority vote. Anwar (1986) estimated that in 1987 there were sixty constituencies in which more than 15 per cent of the population belonged to ethnic minorities.

All available survey evidence shows that ethnic minority voters strongly prefer the Labour party (see Anwar, 1986, ch. 5; Layton-Henry, 1988). For example, a survey by the Commission for Racial Equality in 1983 found that 43 per cent of their white respondents voted Labour compared with 86 per cent of Afro-Caribbeans and 80 per cent of Asians.[12] In 1987, about 67 per cent of Asians and 86 per cent of Afro-Caribbeans voted Labour (Messina, 1989, p. 152). This high level of Labour support is partly explicable in class terms. Voters of West Indian origin in particular are heavily working class. But Labour also attracts support from the ethnic minorities — especially Asians — because it is seen as more liberal in matters relating to race and immigration.

It remains the case, however, that ethnic minority voters constitute a small minority (about 5 per cent) of the total electorate. As a result, representative samples of the whole electorate contain too few of them for separate analysis. In addition, despite the impressively high levels of ethnic minority support for Labour, race remains a weak predictor of party choice because, of course, it does not discriminate among the large white majority.

Finally, in Chapter 2 I reproduced a table from Butler and Stokes which was designed to show the extent to which voters' party preferences were inherited from their parents. Table 3.12 repeats the analysis using 1987 data. Even in this restricted table

Table 3.12 The influence of parents' partisanship on party identification, 1987 (%).

	Both parents Conservative	Parents divided	Both parents Labour
No party identification	9	11	12
Conservative	69	42	21
Labour	9	24	51
Liberal Democrat	12	21	14
Other	1	1	1

Note: 'Divided' means that one parent was Conservative and the other Labour.
Source: 1987 BES cross-section survey.

the influence of parents appears to have been much reduced compared with the 1960s, especially in the case of people with Labour-supporting parents, only half of whom were Labour identifiers in 1987. A fuller analysis of the data shows that only 65 per cent of respondents had parents who both supported one of the major parties, so that the role of the family in establishing party identities seems to be less important than it used to be.

Conclusion

Richard Rose and Ian McAllister (1986, 1990) have developed a model of British voting behaviour which they call a model of 'lifetime learning'. They use multiple regression to trace the extent to which various factors successfully predict party choice at elections from 1964 to 1987 and their analysis helps to pull together the various strands of this chapter. Taken together, occupational class, age, sex, religion, housing tenure and parents' partisanship accounted for 20.7 per cent of the variation in individual party choice in 1964 and 16.4 per cent in 1987. Overall, then, there was a clear decline in the ability of social background variables to predict party choice.

This supports the conclusion that from the 1970s the British electorate, on the whole, moved from aligned to dealigned voting. This is not to say that voters became entirely free-floating, as it were. Rather, there was a marked diminution in the intensity of psychological commitment to the two parties which had previously dominated elections, and in the strength of the relationship between an individual's position in the social structure and his or her party choice. Although new cleavages have emerged, like race, and others continue to be important, like region, voting is no longer so firmly anchored in the social structure. The success rate that one would achieve in predicting party choice from knowledge of a person's class, age, sex or religion has steadily fallen. There still remains *some* alignment but its most striking feature is its weakness, not its strength.

This immediately raises a question. If voters no longer receive powerful cues about which party to support from a long-standing party identification or from their social location, how do they now decide? Some answers to this question are considered in the next two chapters.

Notes

1. Miller, Tagg and Britto (1986) suggest that dealignment began to affect Labour voters in the late 1960s and Conservative supporters between 1970 and 1974.
2. There is some confusion in the early literature on the subject over the precise meaning to be attached to the term 'partisan alignment', and the distinction to be made between this and 'class alignment'. There is general agreement, however, that weakening party identification is a sign of partisan dealignment. It seems logical, therefore, to use 'partisan alignment' to refer to a situation in which voters align themselves psychologically with parties by identifying with them. Such a situation could, of course, exist without an accompanying class alignment.
3. This phrase was used of political parties a long time ago by Graham Wallas (1910).
4. The popularity of David Steel, the Leader of the Liberal party, fell sharply between 1983 and 1987, and many people attributed this in part to the way he was portrayed in *Spitting Image* — as fawning upon and being treated with derision by the Leader of the SDP, David Owen.
5. For a discussion of leadership popularity, see Brown (1992).
6. In this case, of course, we would subtract the percentage Conservative among manual workers from the percentage Conservative among non-manuals.
7. The figures for absolute class voting in Table 3.4 slightly overstate its extent since people who voted for 'other' parties are excluded from the calculations. It is also worth bearing in mind that if non-voters were included in the calculations, the figures for absolute class voting would be substantially smaller.
8. Heath *et al.* also used log-linear analysis in their original study but reported the results only in footnotes.
9. The polling company MORI has conducted panel surveys for *The Sunday Times* at each election since 1979. It is difficult to summarise these data but it is worth noting that during the 1992 campaign the amount of movement found among the electorate was greater than ever before (see Fallon and Worcester, 1992).
10. The changes were from 'How long ago did you decide to vote that way?' to 'How long ago did you decide that you would *definitely* vote the way you did?' and from 'Did you think of voting for any other party?' to 'Was there any time during the election campaign when you *seriously* thought you might vote for another party?'
11. They do not give similar calculations for voters who are not in the salariat.
12. The relevant survey was conducted in mainly Labour-held constituencies.

4

ISSUE VOTING

If a political commentator or politician of the 1920s or 1930s were able to read the previous two chapters, he or she would be utterly amazed at the relative lack of attention paid to party policies or to topical events and political issues. Before survey studies of voting behaviour began, elections and voting were conceived of in terms of choices between competing sets of policy proposals. The voter was pictured as weighing up the policies of the different parties, and on that basis deciding which party to vote for. The party that won an election was thought to have a 'mandate' from the electorate for all of its policy proposals detailed in its election manifesto. In the nineteenth century John Stuart Mill (1963, pp. 302–4) said this about the voter:

> His vote is not a thing in which he has an option . . . he is bound to give it according to his best and his most conscientious opinion of the public good . . . the voter is under an absolute moral obligation to consider the interest of the public, not his private advantage, and give his vote to the best of his judgement exactly as he would be bound to do if he were the sole voter and the election depended upon him alone.

This idealised view of the voter informed much comment upon elections until well into the twentieth century.

In the first two chapters, in contrast, I have considered voting behaviour as almost entirely a function of social and even psychological processes, hardly mentioning party policies or 'the interest of the public'. It would, of course, be going too far to claim that before 1970 not a single voter decided how to vote after carefully evaluating the parties' policies or that policy considerations played no part at all in the decision processes of most voters. The Michigan model explicitly contains 'issue orientation' as a short-term factor affecting party choice and most studies of British voters found that they did have generalised images of the parties that were not without policy content. Thus the Labour party was widely perceived as the party that was 'for the working class' or in favour of nationalisation and higher welfare spending. None the less, when researchers tried to be more precise about the effects of electors' political opinions upon their voting choices, their results did not suggest that there was a very strong connection between the two.

Conditions for issue voting

Following Butler and Stokes (1974), there are four conditions that must be met if an issue is to affect voting and a voter is to qualify as an 'issue voter':

1. The voter must be aware of the issue concerned. Clearly if someone failed to notice that in 1993 the government announced plans to extend VAT to domestic heating fuel then that policy could not affect his or her vote in a subsequent election.
2. The voter must have some attitude towards or opinion about the issue. I might be well aware that people have strong views about whether or not fox hunting should be banned but be completely indifferent myself, or else unable to make up my mind on the question. In these cases the issue could not affect my vote.
3. The voter must perceive different parties as having different policies on the issue. Again, if this is not the case, there is no logical way in which the voter's opinion on the issue can be related to the choice of a party in an election. In the 1960s, for example, many voters had strong opinions on the question of immigration but believed that there was no difference

between the parties on the issue. As a result, the issue did not, on the whole, affect voting behaviour (see Butler and Stokes, 1974, pp. 303–8).

4. Finally, and obviously, the voter must vote for the party whose position on the issue is, or is perceived to be, closest to his or her own position.

Two further points about the role of issue opinions in elections should be noted. First, the four conditions need to apply for an individual to be an issue voter, but for an issue to affect the outcome of an election, many voters have to fulfil the conditions and, in addition, opinion on the issue must be skewed. If roughly the same number of people are for and against some policy, and vote on that basis, the policy will make little difference to the net strength of the parties. If, however, one side of the issue has much greater support than the other, and the other conditions are met, then the overall election result will be altered by the issue.

Second, the kinds of issues that I have had in mind here are 'position' issues. People take positions for and against fox hunting, capital punishment, unilateral nuclear disarmament or whatever (although, of course, on many issues there are more than two possible positions). As Butler and Stokes (1974, p. 292) point out, however, there are many issues on which there is broad agreement among the electorate about the goals that government should pursue. What is at issue is the competence or performance of the parties in seeking to achieve these goals. Not many people, for example, are in favour of increased crime or against peace and prosperity but there would be disagreement about which party would be most likely to be successful in combating the former and promoting the latter. Butler and Stokes called these sorts of issues 'valence' issues and in a later piece Stokes (1992) argues that valence concerns have become increasingly important in elections.

Issue voting in the era of alignment

When aligned voting was the norm in Britain, relatively few voters qualified as issue voters. First, on the question of awareness of issues, studies consistently found that large numbers of electors managed to get through life with only the haziest notion about the

nature of the issues exercising the interest of MPs, political journalists and lobby correspondents, and little understanding of the
language in which political debate was conducted. Butler and
Stokes commented that

> the simplest evidence about the extent of popular attention to the
> affairs of government must challenge any image of the elector as an
> informed spectator. Understanding of policy issues falls away very
> sharply indeed as we move outwards from those at the heart of
> political decision-making to the public at large. (1974, p. 277)

In 1964, 40 per cent of respondents to the BES survey were unable
to name two important questions facing the country (quoted in
Franklin, 1985, p. 128). Politics and political issues were simply
peripheral to most people's concerns.

Butler and Stokes also cast doubt on the extent to which, even
when they were aware of issues and were prepared to nominate the
position they held, electors actually had genuine attitudes towards
issues and policies. They illustrate this by reference to the question
of nationalisation. This is an issue that had been at the centre of
political controversy in Britain for a long time and on which there
were clearly perceived differences between the parties. Yet over
four separate interviews, less than half (43 per cent) of Butler and
Stokes' respondents were consistent in either supporting or opposing further nationalisation. In addition, when Butler and Stokes
investigated the extent to which voters' opinions on eight different
issues were interrelated, they found that opinions did not 'hang
together' in the way that a sophisticated observer would expect.
Thus, opinions on whether trade unions had too much power were
not systematically related to opinions about whether big business
was too powerful. Even when they restricted their analysis to respondents who had constant opinions over time on each issue —
only 30 per cent of the sample — Butler and Stokes concluded that

> the main impression left . . . is of the weakness of the links between
> attitudes . . . even when we go to such lengths to confine our atten-
> tion to the minority of people who have well-formed and enduring
> views, the association of attitudes is relatively feeble. (p. 320)

Perception of differences between the parties on issues (the third
condition for issue voting) varied very much depending upon the
nature of the issue. On 'big' or broad issues, like welfare spending

or nationalisation, voters were mostly able to see a difference between the Conservatives and Labour, but on a whole series of more precise, technical or esoteric policy questions (and on immigration, as noted earlier), this was not the case. In addition, voters were notably unable to assign policy stances to the Liberals.

Finally, even voters who successfully passed the first three issue-voting tests frequently fell at the last fence. Despite having an opinion that they knew was contrary to a party's policy, some would nevertheless go ahead and vote for that party. This was particularly true of Labour supporters, a majority of whom were regularly found to oppose the party's policy of nationalisation. A survey of Bristol voters in 1955 (Milne and MacKenzie, 1958) found that 39 per cent of Labour voters were pro-Conservative in their policy preferences, with a further 27 per cent being neutral.

In sum, then, voting in the era of alignment can fairly be described as virtually 'issueless'. Voters were as likely to change their policy preferences to fit their party as they were to change their party to fit their policy position. There was, of course, *some* issue content in voting decisions and some electors were, no doubt, fully fledged issue voters. But using the criteria suggested by Butler and Stokes, issue voting was the exception rather than the rule. To that extent, voting studies were justified in emphasising the social and psychological bases of voting behaviour.

We have seen, however, that the social underpinnings of party choice have crumbled and partisan attachment has weakened. In these circumstances, issue voting has grown in importance. Some of the factors explaining partisan dealignment — such as increased political awareness and exposure to politics on television — have also increased the propensity of electors to vote on the basis of their policy preferences.

This is not as straightforward as it might appear, however. As more and more attention has been paid to the role of issues in elections, doubts and disagreements have emerged about the meaning and measurement of issue voting.

Measuring issue voting

There is no consensus about what issue voting should be called. The terms used include 'policy voting', 'consumer voting', 'instrumental voting' and 'ideological voting'. Two variants on the basic model are 'investment voting' and 'retrospective voting'. All of these are inspired, in part at least, by rational choice theory (see Downs, 1957), and involve the voter making a calculated decision about which party to support (or even about whether to vote at all) on the basis of his or her policy preferences and assessments of the parties' positions or performance.

The increased concern with issue voting on the part of re-searchers has focused attention upon two important methodological difficulties. The first relates to the problem of causation. If we find that there is a positive relationship between voters' policy opinions and their choice of party, then at least two interpretations of this are possible. The first, based on the 'partisan alignment' model, suggests that voters base their party choice on factors such as their class location or family tradition. In so far as they have policy opinions, these are formed by following the lead of the party. Thus, a voter who is a lifelong Labour supporter would tell a survey interviewer that he or she supports Labour policy on taxation — whatever that policy may be. The issue voting model sug-gests, on the other hand, that long-term influences on voters are relatively weak and that they consider the policies of the various parties and make their decision on that basis. The problem is that showing that there is a strong correlation between issue positions and party choice does not tell us which of these models is operat-ing. It shows that there is a relationship between opinions and vote, but tells us nothing about the processes by which the two come to be related. There is no simple way of resolving the prob-lem of causal direction empirically. We can demonstrate the extent to which voters fulfil the conditions for issue voting, but ultimately it cannot be proved that issue preferences cause or determine party choice.

The second methodological problem is sometimes referred to as the problem of 'decision rules' or 'trade-offs'. A voter might be pro-Conservative on some issues (say, privatisation), pro-Labour on others (say, welfare spending) and pro-Liberal Democrat on others (reforming the electoral system, perhaps). The difficulty is that we do not know how the issue voter decides which issues are the ones that will determine his or her vote. How does a voter 'trade off' a preference for changing the electoral system against a preference for privatising nationalised industries?

The problem can be illustrated from the 1992 BES survey. There were 1,009 respondents to the survey who agreed with the view that the government should introduce stricter laws to regulate trade unions — a Conservative policy. But almost a third (29 per cent) of these respondents also inclined to the view that taxes should be increased a lot to pay for increased spending on health and social services, which is a Labour position, and 44 per cent of them favoured the introduction of proportional representation (a Liberal Democrat policy). Sixteen per cent of those who preferred the Conservative position on trade unions preferred Labour on taxation *and* the Liberal Democrats on electoral reform. Clearly, many people's policy preferences do not all point in the same direction.

The most common way out of this problem is simply to tot up the balance of voters' preferences over a number of issues. But this is not entirely satisfactory, since it involves imposing a decision rule under which all issues are weighted equally, when in reality a voter's opinion on one issue may outweigh his or her preferences on all others.

Evidence of issue voting after 1970

In a series of reports on general elections Ivor Crewe (1981a, 1985b, 1992a, 1992b) has developed a distinctive and simple way of analysing issue voting. This involves, first, the *salience* of different issues, that is, the extent to which they are in people's minds. This is indicated by the percentage of voters mentioning an issue as one that they thought important when they were deciding how to vote. Second, there is the *party preferred* on the issue — the party that is thought to have the best policy. The third factor is the *credibility* of party proposals — the extent to which voters believe that parties will or will not be able to achieve their policy goals.

Table 4.1 shows the figures that Crewe has presented on issue salience and party preference on issues for the last five elections. One fascinating feature of the table is the way in which it charts the rise and fall of various issues. Unemployment is the only one to appear in all five elections. The Common Market, on the other hand, has now disappeared as an issue. Defence policy was salient only in the 1983 and 1987 elections while the NHS and education

Table 4.1   Issues in elections, 1979–92.

	Oct. 1974		1979	
	Salience	Preferred party lead	Salience	Preferred party lead
Prices	82	Lab. +11	42	Lab. +13
Unemployment	12	Lab. +19	27	Lab. +15
Trade unions/strikes	15	Lab. +33	20	Con. +15
Common Market	11	Con. +3	–	–
Taxes	–	–	21	Con. +61
Law and order	–	–	11	Con. +27

	1983		1987	
	Salience	Preferred party lead	Salience	Preferred party lead
Unemployment	72	Lab. +16	49	Lab. +34
Defence	38	Con. +54	35	Con. +63
NHS	38	Lab. +46	33	Lab. +49
Prices	20	Con. +40	–	–
Education	–	–	19	Lab. +15

	1992	
	Salience	Preferred party lead
NHS	41	Lab. +34
Unemployment	36	Lab. +26
Education	23	Lab. +23
Prices	11	Con. +59
Taxation	10	Con. +72
Defence	3	Con. +86

Note: The table reports issues mentioned by more than 10% of voters at any of the elections. The preferred party lead is % saying that the party most preferred on the issue had the best policy minus % saying the same of the next most preferred party.
Sources: Gallup data reported in Crewe (1981a, 1985b, 1992a, 1992b).

appear to have become more significant issues in recent elections. Crewe's contention is that the outcomes of these elections can largely be explained by a combination of changes in the salience of issues and changes in the electorate's judgements about the party that has the best policies on the issues, together with voters' assessments of the credibility of party policies.

In October 1974, Labour was clearly ahead on three of the four major issues and won the election. In 1979, the Conservatives pushed taxation and law and order onto the election agenda and recorded huge leads on these issues. In addition, the electorate's firm preference for Labour on trade union matters in 1974 changed to a preference for the Conservatives in 1979 and, although Labour still led on prices, this issue had become much less salient. This combination was enough to win the election for the Conservatives. Crewe concludes that in 1979 'it was issues that won the election for the Conservatives . . . the Conservatives' success came from saying the right things about the right issues' (1981a, pp. 282–3).

In the 1983 election, unemployment was the most salient issue and Labour was the preferred party on the problem. But Crewe found that Labour's credibility was weak — the voters did not think that Labour could achieve what they actually promised on unemployment. Their lead on this issue and on the NHS was outweighed by large Conservative leads on defence policy and prices.

This line of analysis runs into difficulties, however, when it is applied to the 1987 election. Labour had a clear lead on three of the four most salient issues — unemployment, NHS and education. Despite the enormous Conservative lead on defence, if electors had voted on the basis of their preferences on these issues, Labour would have won the election — but, of course, they lost decisively. In attempting to resolve this paradox Crewe shifts his ground somewhat as compared with his previous analyses. He argues that in 1987 voters were mainly concerned with their own private prosperity and the Conservatives were seen as the party most likely to create or maintain prosperity. 'Here,' says Crewe, 'quite simply and obviously, lies the key to Conservative victory'(1992a, p. 352).

Issue voting is still implicit in this argument but the issue concerned, prosperity, is a valence issue. Prosperity is not a 'problem' but a goal and the voters opted for the party that they judged most likely to attain it. I mentioned 'investment' voting earlier and this is an example of it. The voters, according to Crewe, invested in future prosperity after calculating which party was likely to yield the best return. There is, too, some 'retrospective' element since expectations about the future are to some extent based on experience of the past performances of the parties.

On the face of it, 1992 presents further problems for Crewe's analysis. Labour was well ahead on the top three issues but lost the election. As Crewe points out, however, Labour's advantage on unemployment and health was actually less than it had been in

1987 and, although defence almost slipped off the agenda, the Conservatives gained from the salience of prices and taxation. In addition, Labour again suffered from a credibility problem in that voters did not trust their competence in handling the economy.

Crewe's method of analysing issue voting in these reports has been severely criticised. The survey question used to find out which party a respondent prefers on an issue is some variant of 'Which party do you think would be best at dealing with . . . (the issue concerned)?' This is a heavily loaded question, in that if people are going to vote for a particular party, they are likely to say that it is best on practically anything, without necessarily even knowing what the party's policies are. In Crewe's defence, it could be said that the fact that different parties are preferred on different issues casts doubt on this argument. In any event, Crewe's election reports are not intended to be rigorous tests of the issue voting model but explanations of the outcomes of particular elections.

Fortunately Crewe, together with Bo Sarlvik, has provided a much more exhaustive analysis of issue voting in the 1970s (Sarlvik

Table 4.2   Issue opinions and party choice in the 1979 general election.

	% who have position	% who locate Con. and Lab. dif- ferently	Corre- lation opinion/ party (a)	Corre- lation opinion/ party (b)	Corre- lation opinion/ party (c)
Tax cuts v. govt services	87	80	0.25	0.33	0.44
How to tackle unemployment	85	82	0.35	0.42	0.46
Incomes policy	87	73	0.00	0.32	0.42
Laws to regulate trade unions	87	83	0.41	0.47	0.62
EC economic policies	80	66	0.11	0.24	0.47
Improving race relations	87	70	0.07	0.19	0.36
Social services	98	83	0.28	0.39	0.51
Nationalisation	94	88	0.45	0.48	0.60

Notes: The correlations shown between issue opinion and party choice in column (b) refer to voting for the 'closest' party, as explained in the text. Those given in column (c) are for voters who considered the issue 'extremely important'. The coefficients are Tau-b coefficients which have essentially the same meaning as the correlation coefficient discussed in Chapter 1.

Source: Sarlvik and Crewe (1983, pp. 190–1, 208–9, 213, 217, 223).

and Crewe, 1983). The complexity and extensiveness of their analysis make it difficult to summarise, but for our purposes a number of points stand out. The relevant data are presented in Tables 4.2 and 4.3.

Sarlvik and Crewe analysed opinions on six issues (the first six shown in Table 4.2) by asking respondents to choose between two policy alternatives in each case. In the cases of the two other issues (social services and nationalisation), four alternatives were offered. The first column in the table relates to the first two conditions for issue voting — there must be an awareness of the issue and the voter must have some position on it. Clearly, very large majorities nominated their policy preferences in each case, the lowest being 80 per cent on how Britain should respond to EC economic policies. The third step in the issue voting model — perceiving the parties as having different positions — is tested in the second column. On three issues (incomes policy, reaction to EC policies and improving race relations) the percentage of respondents able to differentiate the Conservative and Labour parties' positions is somewhat smaller than in the other cases. This is not surprising since the parties' positions themselves were not entirely clear. Overall, substantial majorities pass the third condition for issue voting.

The third column of the table concerns the relationships between peoples' opinions on policy and their vote — whether it was Conservative, Liberal or Labour. Correlation coefficients are used to measure this (see Chapter 1) and it is clear that although opinions on some issues are poor predictors of party choice (incomes policy, the EC and race relations), the others show significant positive relationships. That is, policy opinions are clearly related to party choice.

This is not, however, strictly what is meant by issue voting. What we need to know is the extent to which people vote for the party that they *believe is closest* to their view on the issue concerned. Sarlvik and Crewe asked their respondents to indicate what position they thought the various parties took on the issues concerned, and the correlations between opinion and voting for the 'closest' party in this sense are shown in the fourth column of the table and in every case the coefficients are larger than those in the third column.

Finally, Sarlvik and Crewe tackle the problem of 'decision rules' discussed earlier. They group respondents according to their rating of each issue as 'extremely important', 'fairly important' or 'not very important', and find that for each issue the correlations between issue position and party choice are regularly strongest among respondents who consider the issue extremely important and weakest among those who consider it not very important. The figures for those who rate each issue as 'extremely important' are given in the fifth column of Table 4.2, and they are sharply higher than the corresponding figures for all respondents shown in the third column.

Unfortunately, Sarlvik and Crewe do not provide figures for 'closest party' voting, taking account of the importance attached to the issue, but the presumption must be that these correlations would be stronger still. They do, however, consider the combined impact of issue opinions by means of a multiple regression analysis. Taking all eight issues together produces a multiple correlation coefficient of 0.68 between issue opinion and party choice.

Another part of Sarlvik and Crewe's analysis concerns four valence issues — strikes, unemployment, prices and law and order. These are valence issues since few people would actually favour more strikes, heavier unemployment, higher prices or public disorder, and what issue voters do in these cases is assess the relative competence of the parties in handling these problems. As Table 4.3 shows, almost all respondents in 1979 were willing to offer assessments of the ability of the Conservative and Labour parties to handle the problems. The correlations between these assessments and party choice are consistently strong (although stronger

Table 4.3   Valence issues and party choice in the 1979 general election.

	Average % assessing Con. and Lab.	Correlation assessment/party (a)	Correlation assessment/party (b)
Strikes	96	0.52	0.53
Rising prices	97	0.52	0.60
Unemployment	95	0.51	0.56
Law and order	96	0.39	0.44

Notes: The correlations given in column (b) are for respondents who considered the problem 'extremely important'. As in Table 4.2, the coefficients are Tau-b coefficients.

Source: Sarlvik and Crewe (1983, pp. 154–6, 161, 223).

in the case of economy-related issues than for law and order) and they increase in strength when only those who thought an area 'extremely important' are considered. Combining assessments on prices, strikes and unemployment produced a multiple r of 0.69.

Now, what do all these statistics mean? On the basis of this summary of Sarlvik and Crewe's work it is difficult to judge exactly how important issue opinions are in determining party choice, but two further points from their study put issue voting into perspective and give a clearer indication of its importance. First, comparing the effect of policy opinions and assessments with the effect of social characteristics on party choice, they say that 'the voters' opinions on policies and on the parties' performances in office "explain" more than twice as much as all the social and economic characteristics taken together' (p.113). Second, using a statistical technique known as discriminant analysis, they find that the votes of 69 per cent of their respondents can be correctly predicted on the basis of their issue opinions and assessments. If only those predicted to vote for the two major parties are considered (it is notoriously difficult to predict third-party voting), 86 per cent of respondents actually voted for the party that was predicted on the basis of their political opinions.

Critics of issue voting

If 'aligned voting' was the orthodoxy of electoral analysis in the 1950s and 1960s, issue voting has been the orthodoxy of the 1970s and 1980s. All orthodoxies invite challenge, however, and proponents of the issue voting model have themselves come in for criticism.

Heath, Jowell and Curtice (1985) again cast themselves as revisionists. In *How Britain Votes*, they describe issue voting as a 'vogue' and, in a remarkably brief chapter, dismiss the argument that people vote on the basis of their policy opinions. Their conception of issue voting, which they call 'consumer' voting, is, however, very narrow. They describe it as relating to 'the detailed stands which competing parties take on issues of the day' (p. 89), 'detailed appraisals of party manifestos and policies' (p. 99) and 'the small print of the manifesto' (p. 107). Few of those who argue that there has been an increase in issue voting would conceive of it in these terms.

Heath *et al.* criticise the practice of voting analysts in using voters' judgements about the performance or competence of parties to measure issue voting, on the grounds that these judgements are inextricably bound up with party preference. If Labour voters think Labour is best at dealing with unemployment, this is because they are Labour voters. The judgement is a consequence of the party choice, not a cause of it. Heath *et al.* therefore concentrate on position issues. But because they see no logic in imposing a 'decision rule' about the weight attached to different issues, they do not attempt to construct any kind of index that would summarise a person's issue preferences and then see how this relates to his or her party choice. Rather, they show that if people had voted in the 1983 general election for the party that they saw as closest to them on the issue they considered most important, the election would have resulted in a dead-heat between Labour and the Conservatives. Since Labour was in fact trounced, Heath *et al.* argue, the policy voting model can be rejected.

A better model, they suggest, is what might be called 'ideological voting'. Voters do not choose a party on the basis of policy preferences, but on the basis of their 'general values and their overall perceptions of what the parties stand for' (p. 107). To demonstrate the existence and role of these general values, Heath *et al.* use answers to questions about issues and policies. The issues that they find to be most important in differentiating between Conservative and Labour supporters are nationalisation, trade union legislation, income redistribution, defence spending, private education and job creation (p. 109). Not all of these were campaign issues in 1983, say Heath *et al.*, but rather they are bound up with the overall images of the parties and 'constitute the main ideological divisions between the parties' (p. 109). The Labour party, for example, is recognised as the party favouring nationalisation, the trade unions, equality and so on, irrespective of the particular issues of the day. So, while they utilise responses to issue questions, Heath *et al.* see these as 'not so much tapping discrete issues as a general ideological dimension' (p. 111), although they do not present any evidence that people's opinions on these issues intercorrelate in a way that would be expected if they did indeed subscribe to a set of general values.

A somewhat similar account to that given by Heath *et al.* was put forward by Rose and McAllister (1986) after the 1983 election.

They too reject the view that issues, which they define as 'topical issues of the moment, which are transitory by definition' (p. 117), are an important influence on voting behaviour. They say (p. 147) that 'how a person votes is a poor guide to what a person thinks about most issues today' (and, presumably, vice versa). What are important, according to Rose and McAllister, are the 'political principles' that voters hold. Principles are 'underlying judgements and preferences about the activities of government [which] are general enough to be durable ... [and] ... concern persisting problems of public policy' (p. 117).

Rose and McAllister use a technique called *factor analysis* to explore patterns in voters' responses to questions on eleven enduring issues in British politics (such as nationalisation, spending on the health service, etc.) at three separate elections. They identify four principles that appear to underlie opinions and they call these socialism, welfare, traditional morality and racialism. These are distinct principles in the sense that answers to questions dealing with welfare, for example, intercorrelate highly but are not related to opinions in the other three areas.

Only one of Rose and McAllister's principles — socialism — importantly affects party choice. The effect is to penalise Labour since most voters are anti-socialist. The others have only a slight effect on party choice — indeed there is 'intra-party consensus' on them among voters (pp. 124–5).

In their analysis of the 1987 election Heath *et al.* did carry out a more conventional analysis of issue voting and they found that 'in 1983 and 1987 voters' attitudes towards the issues were more closely associated with the way they voted than had been the case in previous election studies. Attitudes have become better predictors of how people will vote' (1991, p. 33). They measure the association using an index of concentration (which is analogous to r^2) and the figures show, using attitudes to topical as well as enduring issues, that the average association was 0.41 for the three elections from 1964 to 1970 and 0.53 for the four elections from October 1974. Heath *et al.* go on to compare the extent to which childhood socialisation has affected Conservative and Labour voting with the effect of childhood socialisation together with current political attitudes. The results are shown in Table 4.4. Clearly the influence of parents declined and that of current opinions increased after 1970.

Table 4.4   Childhood socialisation, attitudes and vote (Con. v. Lab.), 1964–87.

	1964	1966	1970	1979	1983	1987
Parents' party preferences	0.24	0.26	0.29	0.19	0.21	0.19
Parents' party preferences plus respondent's attitudes	0.49	0.46	0.47	0.48	0.59	0.62
Difference	0.25	0.20	0.18	0.29	0.38	0.43

Note: The figures shown are 'indices of concentration' which are analogous to r^2s, giving an estimate of the proportion of variation in party choice explained.
Source: Heath *et al.* (1991, p. 44).

Now, all of this seems good evidence in favour of the view that issue voting increased as the electorate became dealigned. But Heath *et al.* deny that voters are now more influenced by issues. The argument underlying this apparently perverse conclusion is a little complicated but worth setting out in some detail. As mentioned above, finding a correlation between opinions and vote is not enough to show that the issue voting model applies. It could also be consistent with the model of aligned voting. Heath *et al.* suggest that the stronger correlations for later elections simply reflect the fact that political circumstances have changed, not the extent of issue voting. They argue that the strength of the correlation between opinions and vote is related to the extent to which voters see a difference between the parties. If the Conservative and Labour parties move further apart (or are perceived by the electorate as doing so), then a stronger statistical relationship between issue positions and party choice would be expected under the aligned voting model, because those who support their party's policies for the reasons suggested by this model now appear to be more polarised in terms of attitudes. Although there is a stronger correlation between opinions and vote, it is not necessarily the case that voters are more likely to weigh up the issues than they used to be. This, claim Heath *et al.*, is precisely what happened in 1983 and 1987 and they present data showing that their respondents saw a much greater difference between the two main parties in these elections than was the case before. As far as the declining influence of parents is concerned, Heath *et al.* suggest that this is simply due to increased intergenerational social mobility. More people now defect from their parents' party because more are in a different social class from that of their parents, and their voting reflects this.

These are logically sound arguments; but it is worth remembering that stronger correlations between opinions and party choice would *also* be expected if there were increased issue voting as described by proponents of that model. In addition, the point about intergenerational mobility does not fully explain why parental influence should be replaced by the influence of opinions rather than something else.

Heath *et al.* attempt to overcome the problem of the direction of causation between opinions and party choice by looking at trends in perceived party differences. These are certainly suggestive but do not entirely support their interpretation that it is changes in the perceptions of the parties that explain the increasingly strong relationship between attitudes and vote. It is also worth noting that others have tried to show empirically that it is opinions which determine vote and not vice versa. Franklin (1985) uses causal modelling techniques to take account of a variety of factors and concludes that the importance of issues from 1970 onwards was substantially greater than it was before. Denver and Hands (1990) show that even among people who receive no partisan cues from their parents or friends, the relationship between opinions and vote remains strong, and they argue that it is difficult to explain this other than in terms of an issue voting model.

Rose and McAllister (1990) also return to this topic in their later work. Their position is unchanged. They now talk in terms of political 'values' — delineating six economic and six non-economic values — rather than principles, but continue to emphasise the difference between durable political values and opinions on current issues. They say that 'durable political values are more than ten times as important in explaining voting as is the government's handling of issues' (p. 141). It is important to remember, however, that in their model of 'lifetime learning' Rose and McAllister only measure the impact of current issues *after* taking account of family loyalties, socioeconomic interests, political values and the local context. Current opinions are highly intercorrelated with all of these, and so it is not surprising that, once the latter are taken into account, opinions on current issues are found to have little impact.

Judgemental voting

Apart from the important methodological point concerning causation highlighted by Heath *et al.*, the debate about issue voting is really much ado about not very much. The proponents of issue voting are not, for the most part, claiming that voters weigh up every fleeting issue that happens to surface in an election campaign or pore over the small print of election manifestos. Rather, what I — and, I suspect, others — want to argue is that, as the electorate has become more dealigned, voters have become increasingly likely to base their vote upon judgements — whether about current issues, ideologies, leaders or government performance — rather than to make a choice that is a near-automatic response to family tradition and class location. I hesitate to add another term to the profusion that already exists in the issue voting literature, but it might be better to talk in terms of *judgemental voting* rather than issue voting having increased, since this avoids confusion arising from differing definitions of 'issues', 'principles', 'values' or 'ideologies'. Both Heath *et al.*'s ideological voting and Rose and McAllister's 'value' voting can be considered examples of judgemental voting and the latter are in no doubt that voters' opinions have increased in importance in explaining party choice, even after allowing for the effects of social characteristics and parental influence. Their analysis of the 1987 election finds that, taken together, voters' political values — especially economic values — and judgements about the current performances of the parties were easily the most important determinants of party choice, explaining 38.4 per cent of the variation. By contrast, they explained 25.2 per cent of the variation in the 1964 election and were less important then than family influences (see Rose and McAllister, 1990, table 9A).

The economy and voting

Throughout the 1992 American presidential election the communications director of the Clinton campaign hung a sign over his desk which said 'It's the economy, stupid!' This was to remind him that, no matter what happened, the state of the economy was the issue that would win the election for Clinton (and he was proved right). The view that the economy is *the* issue that matters above all others is one that many other politicians and commentators have long shared. Harold Wilson, Prime Minister in the 1960s and early 1970s, believed that 'all political history shows that the standing of a Government and its ability to hold the confidence of the

electorate at a General Election depend on the success of its economic policy' (quoted in Norpoth, 1992, p. 2).

The state of the economy is a classic 'valence' issue. In broad
terms everyone wants prosperity, and few would be opposed to
more specific economic goals such as full employment, stable
prices and increasing real incomes. What is at issue is how well
different parties have performed, or might perform in future, in
delivering these shared goals. In analysing the impact of the state
of the economy upon voting, two distinct approaches have emerged, although the subject matter of both is called 'economic
voting'.[1]

The first uses individual data from surveys and analyses the
effects of voters' opinions about the economy upon their party
choice. The phrase 'opinions about the economy' is rather vague,
and in the course of research two important distinctions relating to
these opinions have emerged. On the one hand, opinions may
involve *retrospective* or *prospective* judgements, and on the other
they may be *sociotropic* or *egocentric*. 'Retrospective' judgements
refer to the past economic performance of governments while
'prospective' judgements concern possible future performance;
'sociotropic' is the term applied to assessments of national economic conditions, while assessments of how the individual concerned has fared, or might fare, are labelled 'egocentric'.

A good deal of research has been undertaken to discover which
combination of economic opinions is most important for voting
behaviour (see Norpoth, 1992). Generally, it has been found that
economic voting is asymmetrical, in that it focuses on the performance of the governing party rather than the opposition and is
more likely to involve punishing a bad performance rather than
rewarding a good one. There is no agreement, however, as to
whether retrospective judgements or prospective evaluations are
more important. Similarly, researchers differ on the relative importance of sociotropic and egocentric evaluations, although
Heath *et al.*'s study of the 1987 election found that the former were
more influential. They concluded that, in the economic sphere,
'individual experiences do not seem to carry as much weight as
collective ones' (p. 142).

A second, and rather different, way of studying 'economic
voting' focuses not on elections but on the period between elections. Using monthly opinion poll reports on voting intentions it is

easy to establish that there is a regular cycle in government popularity which appears between every pair of general elections. Just after an election the winning party enjoys a 'honeymoon' with the voters and its support increases. The government then becomes more and more unpopular but as the next election approaches there is an upswing in support. This cycle is found in by-election results as well as in opinion polls (see Norris, 1990). The question is, to what extent is this electoral cycle related to the actual performance of the economy?

The first statistically advanced attempt to tackle this question in the British context was made by two econometricians (Goodhart and Bhansali, 1970). Using the period 1947–68 they found that a good prediction of the level of government popularity could be obtained using just two economic indicators — the level of unemployment and the rate of inflation. As time passed, however, this simple 'misery index' became less useful. Indeed, if Goodhart and Bhansali's original equation is worked out using 1983 figures for inflation and unemployment, then it suggests that the Conservatives should have received *minus* 156 per cent of the vote in the 1983 election! (see Crewe, 1988, p. 28). Other writers have taken up the topic, however, and produced increasingly complex models of the relationship between government popularity and the health of the economy (see Denver and Hands, 1992, Part III).

Perhaps the best-known model of inter-election government popularity in Britain is one developed by David Sanders and his colleagues (see Sanders *et al.*, 1987; Sanders, 1993). Sanders' innovation is that he does not use objective economic indicators as the basis of his model, but opinion poll results about personal economic expectations.[2] The model is, then, based on *egocentric, prospective* evaluations. It should be stressed that individual respondents' expectations are not matched to their individual voting intention. Rather, the net aggregate level of expectations in each month (the percentage of respondents who think that the financial situation of their household will get worse subtracted from the percentage who think that it will get better) is related to monthly aggregate voting intentions. A simple schematic representation of the model is as follows:

State of   →   Personal economic   →   Level of government
economy   expectations   popularity

Using a relatively simple regression equation based on personal expectations, Sanders (1993) was able to explain over 90 per cent of the variation in government popularity between 1987 and 1990. Further, he found that variations in expectations themselves could in turn be explained by changes in the level of inflation and interest rates and (temporarily) by the introduction of the poll tax. It is worth noting that on this analysis the level of unemployment did not affect levels of party support. The implications of this analysis are clear. Eighteen months before the 1992 election Sanders (1991) suggested that if interest rates and inflation were steadily reduced, personal expectations would become more optimistic and government popularity would recover enough for the Conservatives to win the election. Moreover, he forecast what the Conservative share of the vote would be, given different levels of interest rates and inflation, and these forecasts turned out to be extremely accurate.

Studies of the influence of economic performance and perceptions on levels of party support have become so statistically sophisticated that they are a closed book to most students (and teachers) of electoral analysis. This is a pity, for, as the Sanders example shows, they have produced interesting and important results which not only shed light on the inter-election cycle and why elections are won and lost, but also provide much food for thought by party managers and election strategists. The ultimate failure of Goodhart and Bhansali's model is, however, a reminder that there is no 'last word' in this area. There is no guarantee that models that can explain past electoral cycles will continue to do so. With each new inter-election period, models must be retested and it may be that personal economic expectations will at some point go the way of the 'misery index'.

Conclusion

The decline of the alignment between social-structural characteristics and party choice, as well as the decline of strong party identification, has not left a vacuum in which voters make almost random choices among competing parties. Rather, voting is now structured by opinions. As aligned voting has declined, the 'gap' has been at least partly filled by judgemental voting — especially, perhaps, judgements about governments' handling of the economy. The average British voter of the 1990s (if there is such a person) is strikingly different from the average voter of the 1950s. Today, the voter is more knowledgeable about political issues, more likely to have opinions about them, more aware of the parties' positions on them and more likely to vote (or not vote) for a party on policy or performance grounds.

Notes

1. Heath *et al.* (1991) use the term 'pocket-book' voting. Norpoth (1992) gives an excellent and accessible account of economic voting in Britain using both individual and aggregate data.
2. While personal economic expectations form the core of the model, more sophisticated versions do include objective economic variables, as well as random 'shocks' such as the emergence of a new party leader, the poll tax and so on.

5

PARTY LEADERS, ELECTION CAMPAIGNS AND THE MEDIA

During the 1950 general election campaign the Prime Minister, Clement Attlee, undertook a 1,000-mile tour around Britain. He travelled in his pre-war family saloon car and was accompanied by his wife (who did the driving) and a detective. If they were ahead of schedule they stopped by the roadside and Mrs Attlee would catch up with her knitting while the Prime Minister did a cross-word puzzle (see Nicholas, 1951, pp. 93–4).

The idea of a Prime Minister or major party leader travelling around in this way would be inconceivable today. During modern election campaigns, party leaders are whisked hither and thither by jet, helicopter, battle-bus or car with an entourage of personal staff, security personnel, newspaper reporters, television crews and assorted other hangers-on. This partly reflects the fact that cam-paigns are now focused more on the party leaders. Campaign man-agers have to ensure that the leaders project a good image. Their itineraries are planned in detail, the meetings they address care-fully controlled; they are coached on how to perform well on tele-vision, advised on how to dress, how to have their hair cut, what to say in public speeches and television interviews and so on. Mrs Thatcher even deliberately lowered the pitch of her voice in order to create a more favourable impression upon the voters (Atkinson, 1984, p. 113).

Developments of this kind have led to claims that general elections have become more presidential in character. They are portrayed as contests between candidates for Prime Minister rather than between political parties competing for control of government. Of course, electoral politics have always been personalised to some extent — elections in the second half of the nineteenth century could be portrayed as contests between Gladstone and Disraeli, for example. What is relatively new is the intensive exposure of party leaders on television. What is less clear, however, is what impact party leaders have on election outcomes.

The impact of party leaders

In the previous three chapters I have argued that there has been a major change in electoral behaviour in Britain — from aligned to dealigned voting. On that basis we might expect that there has also been a change in the impact of party leaders.

In the period of alignment, the expectation would be that the personalities of leaders would have had relatively little electoral effect. The original Michigan model did allow for 'candidate orientation' as a short-term influence on party choice but that model was, of course, developed with presidential rather than parliamentary elections in mind. In Britain, the long-term forces of social class and family socialisation would be presumed to have overridden the purely temporary consideration of who happened to be the leader of each party. Indeed, we would expect voters' assessments of the party leaders to have been themselves products of basic party loyalty. On the whole, each party's supporters would have approved of its leader and disapproved of the others.

With the erosion of the importance of long-term factors, however, we might expect an increase in the electoral impact of party leaders. The competence, personality and image of individual leaders might be regarded as akin to issues that could swing votes in the short term.

There are, as might be expected, problems in assessing the precise impact of party leaders. It is difficult to disentangle electors' views about the leader of a party or Prime Minister from views about the party or the government. Judgements of individual politicians will almost certainly be coloured by the political stance of the voter. It seems safe to assume, however, that in the days before extensive television coverage of politics the influence of party leaders on voting was minimal. For the great mass of voters, their only contact with political leaders was through photographs, newspaper reports of speeches and the occasional radio broadcast. It is instructive to note that the first survey study of voting in Britain (Benney, Gray and Pear, 1956) mentions each party leader only once (and then only to report the number of radio broadcasts they made during the election campaign).

By the 1960s, however, political television was well established and the faces, voices and personalities of party leaders became very familiar to voters. Butler and Stokes (1974, ch. 17) found that the Prime Minister and the Leader of the Opposition were highly visible figures about whom most voters had opinions. To assess the electoral impact of leaders, Butler and Stokes compared voters' attitudes to the parties and to the party leaders. They were then able to analyse the voting behaviour of those who were, on balance, favourable to one party but more favourable to the other party's leader. Only relatively small proportions of Butler and Stokes' sample fell into this category — 14 per cent in 1964, 12 per cent in both 1966 and 1970. (The majority of respondents, 55 per cent, 64 per cent and 60 per cent respectively, had favourable attitudes to both a party and its leader; the remainder were neutral towards either parties or leaders.)

Among those who favoured one party but another party's leader, it was attitudes to parties that were decisive. Those who were pro-Conservative in terms of attitude to the parties but pro-Labour in their assessment of leaders, voted Conservative by three to one; those who were pro-Labour in party terms but pro-Conservative in terms of leaders, voted Labour by two to one. None the less, Butler and Stokes did show that party leaders had some impact, especially in the 1970 election. The proportions voting for their favoured party, despite preferring the opposing party's leader, were much smaller than those supporting their preferred party when they also favoured that party's leader. In addition, when voters were balanced or neutral in their attitudes to the parties, but favoured one of the leaders, they tended to vote for that leader's party.

The conclusion reached by Butler and Stokes is judicious. They say that if there is a marked imbalance in the public's estimation of party leaders, if one is clearly preferred or more disliked than another, then that will have some impact on voting choice. This was, indeed, the case in the 1960s when Harold Wilson, the Labour leader, was clearly preferred to Sir Alec Douglas-Home and then to Edward Heath. But even in these cases Butler and Stokes counsel caution. They say that 'the pull of the leaders remains but one among the factors that determine transient shifts of party strength; it is easily outweighed by other issues and events of concern to the public' (p. 368).

Evidence about the impact of party leaders in more recent elections is contained in the series of election commentaries by Ivor Crewe (1981a, 1985b, 1992a, 1992b). In 1979, when the leaders were James Callaghan (Labour), Margaret Thatcher (Conservative) and David Steel (Liberal), the electorate preferred Mr Callaghan as Prime Minister but the Conservatives won the election. Crewe explains this apparent paradox in a clear statement of the standard argument about the role of party leaders in British elections.

> The purpose of general elections is not primarily to choose a party leader to become prime minister but to choose a party to form a government. More importantly, the British electorate tends to vote according to what a party represents rather than who represents the party . . . British voters, if forced to choose between leader and party, tend to abandon the leader. (1981a, pp. 274–5)

Although Mr Callaghan was popular in 1979, Mrs Thatcher was not very unpopular. When not forced to choose between the two, voters gave Mrs Thatcher good ratings. It seems clear, however, that in this election the impact of the leaders was small.

Table 5.1 summarises the electorate's evaluations of the major party leaders at the last three elections. In 1983 Michael Foot was Labour leader and he was a significant electoral handicap. Only 13 per cent of voters thought that Mr Foot would make the best Prime Minister and 63 per cent thought he would be the worst (giving an overall score of –50). Crewe comments: 'Not since the war had a major party leader been regarded as so implausible a prime minister as Michael Foot' (1985b, p. 181). Although Mrs Thatcher was much more popular, she was not an unqualified bonus for the Conservatives. Less than half of the voters believed that she would make the best Prime Minister, and her lead over Mr

Table 5.1   Best and worst person for Prime Minister, 1983–92.

1983		1987		1992	
Thatcher	+21	Thatcher	+8	Major	+30
Foot	–50	Kinnock	–13	Kinnock	–37
Steel	+33	Steel	–2	Ashdown	+5
Jenkins	–4	Owen	+7		

Notes: The figures given are the percentages saying that a leader would make the best Prime Minister minus the percentage saying that he/she would be the worst.
Sources: Crewe (1985b, 1992a, 1992b).

Steel in this respect was not large. Moreover, during her four years in office Mrs Thatcher had aroused a good deal of hostility among some voters, and a quarter thought she would be the worst person for Prime Minister.

There was a clear connection between these perceptions of the major party leaders and voting choice. Among people who voted Labour in 1979 but did not in 1983, Mr. Foot's overall score was –54 and Mrs Thatcher's –8, whereas among those who remained loyal to Labour, Mr Foot scored +34 and Mrs Thatcher –59. Crewe concludes that the party leaders had a negative effect in 1983. Mr Foot, in particular, put people off voting Labour, but hostility to Mrs Thatcher also kept some voters out of the Conservative camp. The lack of positive impact is illustrated by the fact that the popularity enjoyed by Mr Steel (he had the best overall rating) did not enable his party to make a breakthrough.

Comparable figures for the 1987 election are also shown in Table 5.1. (By this time Mr Kinnock was Labour leader and Mr Steel and Dr Owen were joint leaders of the Alliance.) Mrs Thatcher had become more unpopular but was still a net electoral asset to the Conservatives. Mr Kinnock was much more popular than Mr Foot had been, but he was still the most 'popular' choice as worst Prime Minister and he had a negative rating overall. The turnaround in Mr Steel's popularity is difficult to explain (but see Chapter 3, note 4). There was, then, a much smaller imbalance in the electorate's assessment of the two major party leaders than in 1983, and to that extent the impact of the leaders was smaller.

By 1992 Mrs Thatcher had gone and Mr Major was still enjoying something of a honeymoon with the voters. As a result, the gap in popularity between the two major party leaders was significantly greater than it had been in 1987. There is also other indirect evidence that the 'Kinnock factor' harmed Labour. According to Gallup's post-election poll, 22 per cent of voters said that they would have been more likely to vote Labour if John Smith had been party leader, with only 6 per cent saying that this would have made their voting Labour less likely.

A more statistically thorough analysis of the changing impact of party leaders has been undertaken by Anthony Mughan (1993). Mughan uses Gallup data to assess the effect of party leaders, relative to party policies and performance, in elections from 1964 to 1992. Comfortingly for the main argument of this book, he finds that the impact of the party leaders began to increase during the period of partisan dealignment in the mid-1970s and accelerated sharply in 1987 and 1992.

This discussion of evidence from recent elections is far from being an exhaustive analysis of the impact of party leaders. As I suggested earlier, any such analysis would need to try to estimate the electoral effect of leaders independently of such things as party policies and the voter's general political stance, and that is very difficult. On the basis of Mughan's analysis, however, we can conclude that the personalities and images of party leaders have become more important factors in elections as a consequence of dealignment. Even so, it remains the case that the impact of leaders is small unless there is a large difference in how they are regarded by the voters. To avoid significant electoral damage all that parties have to do is to select a leader who is not patently unpopular or perceived to be lacking in competence.

Election campaigns

In Britain the period of the election campaign is legally defined. It must cover at least three weeks before polling day but is usually four weeks long. It is only during the legally defined campaign period that the various rules regulating candidates' spending, broadcasting and other campaign activities apply. This does not mean that parties only campaign in this period — far from it. To some extent, parties are campaigning all the time and, certainly in the year before an election is due (the precise date is determined by the Prime Minister), they clearly engage in what is recognisably campaign activity.

During the formal campaign period, however, there is a massive increase in political activity. Media coverage reaches saturation point with the progress of the campaign being charted day by day. The parties and the politicians expend vast amounts of money and effort in trying to win votes. Campaign strategy teams start work well before the election to plan election broadcasts and press conferences, organise private polls, decide what issues will be emphasised, where the leaders will go, what 'photo opportunities' will be organised and much more. Much professional expertise — including that of famous film directors — is engaged in a modern election campaign. Modern campaigns are also expensive. There is no legal limit on the amount of money that the parties can spend on national campaigning, and in the 1992 election the Conservatives spent about £10 million, Labour about £7 million and the Liberal Democrats about £2 million (Butler and Kavanagh, 1992, p. 260). In addition, the parties receive free time for election broadcasts on television and radio, and every candidate is entitled to a free postal delivery to every elector in his or her constituency.

Does all of this have any effect? Do campaigns swing votes or are they four weeks of 'sound and fury, signifying nothing'?[1] As Pippa Norris says of the 1987 campaign, it is arguable that 'for Labour and the Alliance, no matter how professional the presentation, how effective the grassroots organisation, how persuasive the party political broadcasts, how convincing the leader's speeches, how enthusiastic the rallies, they could not win against the Conservatives' (1987, p. 458). As before, the shift from aligned to dealigned voting provides a framework within which the effects of campaigns can be evaluated.

With aligned voting, the election campaign is merely one other short-term factor that might marginally affect the voters. When the great majority of voters had enduring party loyalties they were unlikely to be deflected from them by any incidents occurring in a short campaign. Compared to the deep-seated influences of class and party identification, campaigns paled into insignificance. As these enduring ties have loosened, however, it seems likely that voters have become more open to influence during campaigns. Fewer will have their minds already made up when the campaign begins.

Some support for this interpretation has already been seen in Table 3.7 which charted an increase in 'campaign swithering' since 1964. During the 1992 election, the MORI/*Sunday Times* panel polls found that only 63 per cent of respondents had their minds made up before the election was called, 21 per cent made their decision in the last week of the campaign and 8 per cent in the last twenty-four hours. These figures are certainly consistent with the view that there are plenty of voters 'up for grabs' during campaigns.

Given the fact that there are now almost daily opinion poll reports of voting intentions it is relatively easy to trace the level of party support throughout election campaigns. Figure 5.1 shows the trends in the 1992 election. What is striking is the stability of party support. By the end of the campaign the three major parties were close to the points at which they stood at the outset. But this does not mean that the campaign made no difference. Party campaigns have three main aims — to *reinforce* voters who are inclined to support them but who may be wavering or not strongly committed, to *recruit* people who are genuinely undecided at the start of the campaign and to *convert* those who start off with a preference for another party.[2] Campaign panel polls show that a good deal of this does happen — especially recruitment from indecision. If, however, no one party does much better than the others then the effects of all the campaign movements will be to leave the net levels of party support relatively unchanged. In other words, aggregate stability can conceal and be a product of much individual change. This is what appears to have happened in both 1987 and 1992. In 1983, however, during the last two and a half weeks of the campaign individual changes markedly disfavoured Labour and the result was that there was a steady decline in overall support for Labour and an increase in the Alliance's share of voting intentions, to the extent that the latter almost snatched second place.

Thus far, I have discussed election campaigns in a general way. For more detailed consideration we need to distinguish two levels of campaigning. On the one hand, there are local campaigns. In every constituency candidates and party workers put up posters, deliver leaflets, canvass voters, hold meetings, make statements to the local press and try to get their supporters to the polls on election day. Ordinary voters have direct contact with the campaign at this level. On the other hand, there is the national campaign. This is dominated by the party leaderships, with daily press conferences, walkabouts, set-piece addresses to party rallies, election broadcasts and TV interviews. Overwhelmingly, the voters experience this campaign only through the mass media, especially television.

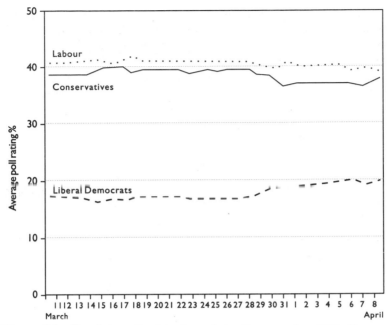

Figure 5.1   Trends in voting intentions during the campaign, 1992. (Source: Butler and Kavanagh, 1992, p. 137.)

Note: The daily figures used are the averages of the results of the previous five or six polls.

Local campaigns

In the 1950s and 1960s, whether they knew it or not, the local campaigning techniques adopted by the political parties were based on the model of stable voting which I outlined in Chapter 2. The main purpose of the campaign was to identify known or likely supporters and ensure that they voted. Each party knew where its supporters were to be found — in council estates and other working-class areas for Labour, in private housing estates and middle-class suburbs for the Tories — and concentrated their attention there. Party workers were actively discouraged from 'wasting time' by trying to persuade opponents or 'doubtful' voters of the merits of their candidate. The underlying assumption was that party loyalties were more or less fixed and the aim of the campaign was to maximise the turn-out of supporters.

Constituency campaigns were not primarily intended, therefore, to alter the party choice of electors, although they were intended to influence the result of an election. Even in this limited respect, however, the general view of electoral analysts has been that constituency campaigns, apart from rare special cases, made no significant difference. There was some evidence that effective campaigning could have a significant impact in local government elections (see Bochel and Denver, 1971), but the consensus was that in general elections local campaigning was little more than an anachronistic ritual.

Many constituency campaigns still largely follow the traditional pattern and voters continue to have direct contact with general election campaigns at local level. During the 1992 campaign, according to MORI figures, 86 per cent of voters had received election leaflets through the door in the previous week and 30 per cent had been canvassed by one of the parties. Gallup's post-election poll found that 43 per cent of voters had read the election address of a local candidate. Attendance at public meetings, once an important feature of election campaigns, is now minimal, however, with only 4 per cent of electors reporting attending a meeting in 1992.

In some respects, however, constituency campaigning is now more sophisticated than it used to be. Extensive use is made of computers; fax machines enable fast and cheap communication between party headquarters and the constituencies, and in well-organised local campaigns attempts are made to target specific groups of voters. It might also be expected that the decline of aligned voting would result in local campaigns having more influence.

There is some indirect evidence that this is the case. It is now fairly common, for example, for there to be massive turnovers of opinion in parliamentary by-elections. But by-elections are atypical in that parties devote great resources to them — bringing in national officials as organisers and party workers from near and far — and the media bring the full glare of national publicity onto an individual constituency in a way that is not possible in a general election. General election results themselves, however, have shown an increasing variability in results from constituency to constituency (see Chapter 6). More individual candidates are able to buck the national trend and it may be that this is a product of local campaigning. In addition, recent elections have seen a good deal of 'tactical' voting in some constituencies. That is, significant numbers of voters have opted for their second-choice party in order to defeat their least-favoured party. Where this happens, local party organisations must play an important part in informing voters of the tactical situation in the constituency and in persuading them of the potential effectiveness of a tactical vote.

None the less, this evidence is fragmentary and the arguments are largely speculative. The authors of the Nuffield study of the 1992 election continue to be sceptical, concluding that 'it is hard to locate evidence of great benefits being reaped by the increasingly sophisticated and computerised local campaigning' (Butler and Kavanagh, 1992, p. 245) while Ivor Crewe declared bluntly during the campaign, 'constituency organisation counts for next to nothing in the television age'.[3]

Some more direct evidence contradicts this orthodoxy. Seyd and Whiteley (1992; see also Whiteley and Seyd, 1992) argue, on the basis of a postal survey of Labour party members, that Labour's performance in both the 1987 and 1992 elections was affected by the strength of its constituency organisations. Denver and Hands (1993) use a survey of election agents to derive a measure of local campaign intensity and conclude that the variations in local campaigning were significantly related to variations in the performance of Labour and the Liberal Democrats across constituencies. It should be emphasised that both of these studies find effects that are *statistically* significant. The authors would not claim that local campaigning is a major influence on election results. It is more a matter of stemming or accentuating a national tide. None the less, we have here another area in which evidence in tune with the kinds of developments anticipated by dealignment theorists is beginning to emerge.

The national campaign

Elections used to be much less 'general' than they are now. In the nineteenth and early twentieth centuries a 'general' election was really a series of individual constituency contests with little central involvement or direction. It was not until 1918 that all constituencies polled on the same day.

The growth of the mass media has changed all this. Elections are now nationwide contests and the national campaign is the dominant focus of attention. Modern campaigns are media campaigns; they are a form of spectator sport. Most people do not participate in them but watch them on television or read about them in the newspapers. As has often been observed, a party leader making an election broadcast today will talk to more people in ten minutes than Gladstone and Disraeli did together throughout their careers.

Since the 1960s, television has utterly dominated national campaigns. The activities of the party leaders are 'media events' especially staged to be reported; 'photo opportunities' are carefully arranged; schedules are timed to fit in with television news coverage. When leading politicians address meetings they do not really speak to their live audiences — who are occasionally glimpsed, glassy-eyed with incomprehension — but to the TV audience who will see clips from the speech ('sound bites') later in the evening. Indeed, speeches are deliberately constructed so that they contain plenty of sound bites for television producers to use.

The extent to which electors follow elections via the media is clear. During the 1992 campaign, 71 per cent of voters reported that they had seen a party election broadcast in the previous week (MORI) and almost everyone must have seen some campaign coverage. Table 5.2 shows that television is said by voters to be their most important source of political information, with newspapers being an important secondary source.

The distinction to be made between the national election campaign and media coverage of the campaign has become increasingly blurred. To all intents and purposes, examining the impact of the national campaign is the same as examining the impact of the mass media upon the voters during the campaign.

Table 5.2   Sources of political information, 1983 (%).

	Most important source	*Top two most important sources*
Television	63	88
Newspapers	29	73
Radio	4	14
Personal contacts	3	12
Other	1	3

Source: Dunleavy and Husbands (1985, p. 11).

Figure 5.2   Direct-effects model of media influence.

The effects of the media

The question of the extent to which people's attitudes, opinions and behaviour are influenced by the mass media, especially television, is one that has provoked an enormous amount of research. Early media theorists, impressed by the apparent power of the media to influence ideas, posited what is called a *direct-effects* or *hypodermic-needle* model. This is illustrated in Figure 5.2. The source or sender (S) communicates information by a particular channel (print or television) to a receiver (R). The receiver receives the message directly, accepts it and is influenced by it.

Empirical research on political attitudes quickly found that this model was far too simplistic (see Trenaman and McQuail, 1961; Blumler and McQuail, 1967). Voters did not come to mass media with blank minds. Rather, they already had opinions, values and experiences which affected their perceptions and interpretations of media messages. The direct-effects model was, therefore, replaced by the *filter* model, which is illustrated in Figure 5.3.

An important psychological theory underlies this model — the theory of *cognitive dissonance*. Cognitive dissonance is a psychological state of unease or tension which occurs when an individual encounters facts or arguments that are at variance with his or her beliefs or attitudes. Subconsciously everyone wants to avoid this, and does so by 'screening out' some information while being

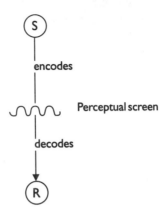

Figure 5.3   Filter model of media influence.

receptive to other information. Generally, people seek reinforcement of their own position from the media, and seek to avoid
communications which contradict their views. This is done in three
ways.

1. *Selective exposure.* We can not read all the newspapers or
   watch all television programmes. We tend to read and watch
   material that supports our political viewpoint, for example.
   Indeed, many people avoid 'political' material altogether and
   concentrate on sport, entertainment, soap operas and so on.
2. *Selective perception.* Even when we come across hostile media material, we reinterpret it to fit in with our preconcep-
   tions or do not even perceive its hostility. As Simon and
   Garfunkel put it a long time ago in a popular song ('The
   Boxer'), 'A man hears what he wants to hear and disregards
   the rest'.
3. *Selective retention.* We remember selectively. We remember
   things that fit in with our views and quickly forget things that
   do not.

People employ these mechanisms subconsciously in 'decoding' the
communications that have been 'encoded' by the sender. In doing

so, they erect a 'communications barrier' or 'perceptual screen' between themselves and the mass media. Despite all the propaganda efforts of the newspapers and of the parties in campaign broadcasts, the main effect of the media as interpreted by this model is to reinforce the voters' existing predispositions.

Television

As we have seen, television is a much more important means of political communication than the press and it now dominates election campaigns. To be a successful party leader these days it is important to 'come over' well on television. However, television coverage of politics is avowedly non-partisan (except, of course, for party political broadcasts). The BBC and the independent television companies are legally obliged to maintain neutrality and balance between parties, and great efforts are made by them to ensure that the major parties receive equal amounts of coverage, especially during campaigns.

The two pioneering studies of the effects of television on British voting behaviour (Trenaman and McQuail, 1961; Blumler and McQuail, 1967) found that, among a variety of sources of political information, only television was able to overcome the 'communications barrier' between people and the media. But it did so only to the extent of increasing the voters' level of political information. It did not change but rather reinforced political attitudes and opinions. The two books provided clear support for the 'filter' model of media effects. Thus, Trenaman and McQuail concluded that 'In the field of attitudes a highly significant screening effect separates exposure to the campaign from changes in strength or direction of attitude' (p. 233). They said that there was 'a definite and consistent barrier between source of communication and movement of attitudes in the political field at the General Election' (p. 192).

Many people find the conclusion that television has little effect on political opinions difficult to accept. It seems to fly in the face of common sense to suggest that such a pervasive medium has little impact upon political attitudes and behaviour. I myself have pointed to increased coverage of politics on television as a source of dealignment (Chapter 3). Moreover, if television has such little impact upon voters, why do the professionals in the political parties assiduously tailor their campaigns to television?

In attempting to resolve this paradox, one preliminary point needs to be made. Both of the studies mentioned — and many others besides — were conducted in situations in which all parties had access to television. Their authors would not deny that if one party had a monopoly, or even a disproportionately large share of television coverage, then the results could be quite different. Parties could not, on the basis of these research findings, simply opt out of campaigning via television and leave the field free to their opponents.

It is also important to remember that both of the studies referred to were completed around thirty years ago. Trenaman and McQuail's book is concerned with the 1959 general election while Blumler and McQuail's deals with the 1964 election. Much has changed since then. The quantity of political coverage on television has greatly increased and its quality has vastly improved: television commentators, interviewers and presenters concerned with political coverage are much more professional.

Another change has been in the party system. When these studies were undertaken, the supremacy of the Conservative and Labour parties was virtually unchallenged. Today, the system is more complex and it is relevant to note that Blumler and McQuail (ch. 11) suggested that a general effect of election broadcasting might be to improve the position of third parties.

A major problem with both studies is that their focus is very much short term. They concentrate on the election campaign period only and on changes in voting intentions and attitudes (rather than, for example, reinforcement or crystallisation). The main reason for their short-term focus is that it is difficult (and expensive) to construct a research programme to study the long-term effects of television. Indeed, it is difficult even to imagine how this could be done since people are constantly exposed to a multiplicity of other influences. None the less, it seems unrealistic to expect to find marked changes in political opinions in such a short space of time, especially in a situation where voting was highly structured by class and party identification. Television's influence could be long-term, slow and subtle — but none the less real. Party election broadcasts might not convert people but that does not mean that attitudes might not be shaped over a long period.

This argument has been put forward in a series of studies by the Glasgow University Media Group (1976, 1980, 1982). These researchers analysed the output of television news broadcasts and concluded that TV news is not neutral in its treatment of stories but displays a consistent bias against left-wing political views. News is reported from a vaguely middle-of-the-road perspective. However, the Glasgow group's concentration upon the *output* of television means that they do not study with any seriousness the *effects* on viewers' opinions of the bias they allege. In addition, the methodology and conclusions of these studies have been severely criticised (see Harrison, 1985).

Perhaps the most important change in the context of political television is the emergence of a more dealigned electorate. This has serious implications for the filter model. It was the existence of party identification which to a large extent created the communications barrier. It was because most voters had strong pre-existing party loyalties that they employed selective processes in response to political messages in the media. If people were strongly Conservative, they would screen out pro-Labour information and remember pro-Conservative information. Since there has been a notable decline in the strength of party identification, it would seem reasonable to infer that the communications barrier has become rather more permeable in recent years.

There has been no full-scale study of the effects of television upon voting behaviour in the period of dealignment. Simple observation suggests, however, that television now plays a much more influential role in campaigns. In particular, its role as agenda-setter is clear. It is television producers and commentators who decide which campaign issues will be discussed and which events reported. Party spokesmen in TV interviews try hard to talk about the issues they want to publicise (usually because they know that these are issues on which the electorate are favourable to their party) but interviewers often relentlessly pursue the topics that *they* think the viewers want to hear about. Miller investigated the effect of television news on public perceptions of the agenda of the 1987 election campaign and found that, while television could only influence what the public thought the parties should be talking about, 'it could dictate public perceptions of the parties' agenda' (1991, p. 165).

The conditions for increased television influence on voting behaviour exist. Party identification, which previously filtered voters' perceptions of political communications, has declined in import-ance. Issue or judgemental voting has become more prevalent and a precondition of this is information. Television is by far the main supplier of political information. Furthermore, voters are now more affected by the personalities and performance of party leaders and this must largely be based on the image projected by leaders on television. It may be, however, that the influence of television is so pervasive, long-term and mixed up with other fac-tors that it is simply beyond the current ability of social science methods to measure it empirically.

The press

The filter model of communication is well illustrated by analysis of the role of the press in influencing political attitudes. The national press in Britain is overwhelmingly and clearly partisan. On elec-tion day in 1992, for example, the whole of the front page of the *Daily Mirror* was taken up with Labour's red rose logo, a picture of Neil Kinnock and the slogan: 'The time is now — vote Labour'. It would be difficult to be more clearly partisan than that! But few readers of this book would have any difficulty in saying which party most national newspapers support. Table 5.3 shows how the papers lined up at the 1992 general election. Perhaps the only surprise was the last-minute decision of the normally Conservative *Financial Times* to advocate a hung parliament with Labour as the largest party.

Table 5.3 Partisanship of the national daily press, 1992.

Conservative		Labour	
The Sun	(3.9)	Daily Mirror	(2.9)
Daily Mail	(1.8)	The Guardian	(0.4)
Daily Express	(1.5)	*Not Conservative*	
Daily Telegraph	(1.0)	Financial Times	(0.3)
The Times	(0.4)	*None*	
Today	(0.3)	Daily Star	(0.8)
		The Independent	(0.4)

Note: The Guardian advocated a Labour victory but also an increased number of Liberal Democrat MPs. Circulation figures (millions) are shown in brackets.
Source: Butler and Kavanagh (1992, pp. 181–2).

There is clearly a strong pro-Conservative bias in national daily newspapers. The circulation of pro-Conservative papers totals 8.9 million: all the rest total only 4.8 million. From time to time, people point to this discrepancy (especially at Labour party conferences) and claim that it accounts for the poor showing of Labour and for Conservative dominance in recent elections. Indeed, after the 1992 election the former Conservative party treasurer, Lord McAlpine, wrote:

> The heroes of this campaign were Sir David English [editor of the *Express*] and Kelvin McKenzie [editor of the *Sun*] and the other editors of the grander Tory press. Never in the past nine elections have they come out so strongly in favour of the Conservatives. Never has the attack on the Labour party been so comprehensive . . . This is how the election was won. (*Sunday Telegraph*, 12 April 1992)

More prosaically, the *Sun* claimed in a headline two days after the election, 'It's *The Sun* wot won it'.

But this is to make a too-simple connection between what the papers say and what the voters do. It is certainly the case that there is a correlation between the papers people read and the party they vote for. Table 5.4 shows the vote of the readers of the various papers in 1992. The relationship is far from perfect — only a minority of the readers of the extravagantly pro-Conservative *Sun* actually voted Conservative, for example, and the surprising preference of the *Financial Times* apparently left its readers unmoved — but it is fairly consistent and clear. Readers of pro-Conservative papers (grouped at the top) all gave the Conservatives a clear lead; readers of the two Labour-supporting papers gave majority support to Labour. Figures similar to these have been reported regularly at British elections.

What is not clear, however, is how these data are to be interpreted. It is not clear whether readers' political views are shaped by the paper they read or whether they choose a paper which is politically congenial to them. People may read the *Guardian* and vote Labour, but that does not mean that they vote Labour because they read the *Guardian*. Rather, they may read the *Guardian* because they vote Labour. In other words, the data may reflect selective exposure.

In fact, this has been the standard interpretation of the relationship between newspaper readership and party choice. In the 1960s,

Table 5.4   Party supported by daily newspaper readers, 1992 (%).

	Conservative	Labour	Liberal Democrat
Sun	45	36	14
Daily Mail	65	15	18
Daily Express	67	15	14
Daily Telegraph	72	11	16
The Times	64	16	19
Today	43	32	23
Daily Mirror	20	64	14
Guardian	15	55	24
Financial Times	65	17	16
Daily Star	31	54	12
Independent	25	37	34

Note: Rows do not total 100 because voting for other parties is not shown.
Source: Butler and Kavanagh (1992, p. 190).

Butler and Stokes (1974) found similar relationships between newspaper reading habits and party choice. They concluded, however, that in general the relationship was a spurious one.

> The correlation is most likely to have been produced by the family's passing on a partisanship which the child has matched by his choice of paper, or by its passing on a more general social location to which both paper and party are appropriate . . . it is clear that newspapers often profit from, rather than shape, their reader's party ties. (p. 118)

Butler and Stokes did find that the press helped to conserve or reinforce party loyalties and had a minor role in creating a party preference where readers were previously uncommitted. But there was little evidence that people switched parties as a result of reading a paper with a particular partisan bias.

A similarly careful analysis of the political effects of reading different newspapers in 1983 is given by Martin Harrop (1986). He too finds some support for the view that papers can help to shape a party preference where readers previously had none, but he concludes that the main effect of the press is the reinforcement of existing party loyalties and finds no consistent evidence that newspapers convert their readers to the party supported by the paper.

These interpretations represent the consensus among political scientists on the role of the press in influencing voting behaviour and are clearly in accordance with the filter model. As with television, however, the weakening of party identification implies that voters could now be more open to persuasion by the press. Since they do not have a strong pre-existing preference for a party, they are less likely to filter information; lacking the 'anchor' of party identification they may be more likely to drift with the tides of opinion in the newspapers that they read. Proponents of the dealignment thesis would predict, therefore, that suitable research would find more positive evidence of press effects than hitherto and such evidence is beginning to emerge.

As noted above, one of the problems that has bedevilled research on media influence is that it has tended to focus very much on the short term. Miller (1991), in the first major post-dealignment analysis of media effects, sought to overcome this problem by reinterviewing the same panel of respondents at widely different points in time. His results may fairly be described as sensational. Over the year between the summer of 1986 and the election of 1987, the change in the Conservatives' lead over Labour among Miller's panel as a whole was +10 per cent. Among readers of the *Express* and *Mail* it was +17 per cent; for *Sun* and *Star* readers it was +34 per cent; while among readers of the *Mirror* it was a mere +2 per cent. This suggests that the tabloids did influence their readers over this period. When Miller breaks down the readers of the different newspapers into those who were committed to a party (party identifiers) and those who were uncommitted, the figures are even more striking. Table 5.5 reports some of his results.

Clearly, the influence of the tabloids was particularly strong among voters who had weak or non-existent commitment to one of

Table 5.5 Change in Conservative lead over Labour, 1986–87.

Among readers of	Politically committed	Uncommitted
No paper	0	+10
Express/Mail	+9	+28
Sun/Star	+10	+50
Mirror	+2	0

Source: Miller (1991, p. 194).

the parties. Readers of the *Sun* and *Star* who were uncommitted to a party seem to have been influenced to a remarkable extent. When it is remembered that levels of political commitment in Britain have steadily declined, the message of these data seems to be that there has been a corresponding increase in the scope for the national press to influence political attitudes and opinions and party choice.

The second set of evidence comes from a piece of secondary research by Kenneth Newton (1991). Newton seeks to overcome the problem of selective exposure — the argument that people choose a paper that reflects their political opinions. He uses BES data to look at the party choice of people who have the same opinions but read different newspapers. The suggestion is that in this way selective exposure can be controlled, and that if people with the same attitudes tend to support the party favoured by their paper, then this would indicate that the press does influence party choice. Newton summarises his results as follows:

> Among those with three typically Conservative attitudes . . . those who read Conservative papers vote Conservative more frequently (96.6 per cent in 1983 and 98.0 per cent in 1987) than those who read Labour papers (89.1 per cent in 1983 and 75.0 per cent in 1987). Among those with Labour attitudes . . . those who read Labour papers vote Labour more frequently (100 per cent in 1983 and 98.9 per cent in 1987) than those who read Conservative papers (91.2 per cent in 1983 and 91.7 per cent in 1987). (1991, p. 63)

Newton's piece is explicitly exploratory — the percentages are sometimes based on rather small numbers of respondents, for instance — but it is an ingenious attempt to get over the problem of selective exposure and his results are in line with Miller's more ambitious study. In both cases, the expectations of dealignment theorists are borne out. The weakening of party identification appears to have allowed the press to have a significant effect upon party choice. It is worth saying again, however, that it is extremely difficult to isolate the effects of one specific factor upon voting behaviour. As well as reading a newspaper, voters are exposed to a multiplicity of other influences upon their opinions — television, family, friends, colleagues at work, being made redundant and so on. It is impossible to control for all of these at once and so measure newspaper influence. We cannot, then, be absolutely certain; but the evidence from recent research suggests that the filter model of press influence no longer gives an adequate interpretation of the effect of press partisanship upon party choice.

Public opinion polls

Public opinion polls are now a familiar aspect of general election campaigns. They are closely related to media campaign coverage, since it is newspapers and television programmes that commission many of the polls, and the voters read and hear about polls in the press and on television. In recent years the number of published campaign polls has increased dramatically. Table 5.6 shows the number of nation-wide polls published during the campaign period in elections since 1970. It should be noted that in addition to the fifty-seven separate nation-wide polls reported in the table for the 1992 election there were also, according to Crewe:

> regional polls in Scotland, Northern Ireland, London and the West Midlands; polls of marginal seats in London, Wales, Yorkshire and the West Midlands; at least 18 individual constituency polls; a four wave panel survey of floating voters; special polls of farmers, teachers, company directors, and Irish and first-time voters; three exit polls on election day; and two post-mortem polls and one post-election poll immediately after. (1992d, p. 475)

It is clearly no exaggeration to say that recent elections have been characterised by 'saturation' polling, and it is not surprising that during the election 73 per cent of voters said that that they had noticed the results of an opinion poll (Gallup, 1992).

Although a number of smaller companies are involved, political polling in Britain is dominated by five major firms — Gallup (the oldest), National Opinion Polls (NOP), International

Table 5.6 Number of nation-wide campaign polls published.

1970	Feb. 1974	Oct. 1974	1979	1983	1987	1992
25	25	27	26	46	54	57

Source: Crewe (1992d).

Table 5.7 Average error in final campaign polls' predictions of major parties'
vote shares.

1964	1966	1970	Feb. 1974	Oct. 1974	1979	1983	1987	1992
1.0	1.7	2.3	1.3	1.7	0.3	1.7	1.7	3.3
(4)	(3)	(5)	(6)	(5)	(5)	(7)	(7)	(4)

Note: The figure for each election is the mean of the differences between the share
of the votes obtained by each of the three major parties and the average share of
the vote forecast for each. The figure in brackets is the number of polls concerned.
Source: Calculated from table 2 in Crewe (1992d).

Communications and Marketing (ICM), Harris, and Market and
Opinion Research International (MORI). These are highly reputable companies and it would be very much against their interests if
any of their clients were to distort their results. There is no question of the media 'fiddling' poll figures. What the polling firms
cannot control, however, is editorial comment or newspaper head-
lines, and sometimes these give a misleading impression of what a
poll has actually found.

Campaign poll results are sometimes portrayed as predictions of
the outcome of the election in question. Strictly speaking, this is
not the case. What campaign polls actually provide is a snapshot of
the electorate's voting intentions at a particular point in time, not a
prediction of how they will vote at a later date. ('Exit' polls are not
strictly campaign polls and their purpose clearly *is* predictive.)
None the less, the polling firms themselves treat their final polls as
election forecasts and it is legitimate to assess the accuracy of polls
by comparing the result of the final poll produced by each company with the actual election result. The accuracy of the polls in
recent elections in this respect is summarised in Table 5.7.

Overall, the record up to 1992 is very creditable. With the exception of 1970, when polling finished some days before the election
and it is generally agreed that there was a swing to the Conservatives in the last few days of the campaign, errors were well within
the margins expected in any poll. The performance is especially
impressive given that not everyone questioned by pollsters actually
turns out to vote, and that, as the electorate has become more
dealigned, pollsters have had to cope with more 'late deciders' and
'waverers', as well as a more fragmented party system. There is,

too, always the possibility that the polls may be self-falsifying, since the publication of their results may alter the very behaviour that they are trying to describe.

In 1992, however, the polls came seriously unstuck. Only one of the four polls published on election day put the Conservatives ahead of Labour and then only very slightly. Exit polls conducted on the day were more accurate but still underestimated the Conservative lead. There have been a number of detailed analyses of why the polls got it wrong on this occasion (Crewe, 1992d; Butler and Kavanagh, 1992, ch. 7) and various suggestions have been made. There may have been a *very* late swing to the Conservatives; the methods used by the pollsters may have been faulty; the electoral register may have been more inaccurate than usual; Conservative supporters may have refused to answer questions or else deliberately lied to interviewers because they were ashamed to admit that they intended to vote Tory; people may have realised that there is a qualitative difference between stating a preference in a poll and actually putting a cross on the ballot paper. As David Sanders (1992) points out, however, it is extremely difficult to determine what really went wrong without using survey-based data, and there is no guarantee that these do not suffer from the very same problems that led to misleading poll predictions.

In one respect, however, the polls can be exonerated. On election night, both television channels used exit polls to predict the outcome of the election in terms of seats in the House of Commons — and in both cases early predictions were very misleading. But what polls attempt to measure is the distribution of party support among the electorate. Extrapolating from this to the distribution of seats in the House of Commons is a tricky business and, given the unpredictability of the electoral system, it is becoming trickier. In February 1974, for example, the party that won most votes (the Conservatives) did not win most seats. In 1987, ITN seriously underestimated the likely Conservative majority in the House of Commons despite the fact that its exit poll, conducted by Harris, got the Conservative lead over Labour in terms of vote share almost exactly right. In 1992, both channels tried to be too clever. Rather than simply using the general exit polls to estimate the numbers of seats that would be won, they took particular account of poll results in marginal seats and made other adjustments, and this is what led them astray.[4]

For my purposes the main question to consider is whether the publication of opinion poll results during election campaigns influences voting behaviour. There have been two main hypotheses in this area — a 'bandwagon' effect and a 'boomerang' or 'underdog' effect. The first suggests that, when one party is seen to be in the lead, some voters will 'jump on the bandwagon' and its support will increase, while supporters of the losing party will lose heart and may not vote. The 'boomerang' hypothesis says exactly the opposite: supporters of the leading party become complacent, and sympathy for the underdog results in an upsurge of support for the trailing party. Clearly both hypotheses cannot be true and in the early 1970s Teer and Spence (1973, ch. 6) concluded that there was no consistent pattern supporting either hypothesis. Crewe (1992d) notes, however, that in six out of the last eight elections the polls have exaggerated the lead of the party that they reported being in the lead. In each case the underdog has done better than expected. He suggests that in 1992 the fact that the polls were uniformly predicting a likely hung parliament probably stiffened the resolve of Conservative waverers.

It is possible that third-party support is influenced by poll results. During the 1983 campaign, Alliance support improved rapidly as polling day approached. Alliance-inclined voters, it could be argued, were encouraged by the first signs of improvement in the polls and switched to the Alliance, thereby producing a sort of 'multiplier' effect. Alliance leaders were, indeed, accused by their opponents of 'talking up' their level of support in the polls in order to achieve just such an effect. After the election Gallup found that, among voters who had seen the results of a poll, 9 per cent of Alliance voters said that their vote had been influenced by the polls, compared with only 2 per cent and 3 per cent of Conservative and Labour voters respectively (Rose, 1985, p. 131). In contrast, during the 1987 and 1992 campaigns the centre parties failed to register any significant increase in support until the very end of the campaign, and this may have dissuaded some potential supporters from voting for them. In all of these cases, however, it is impossible to know whether the polls were creating an effect or merely reflecting what was happening, quite independently, among the electorate. Moreover, no 'multiplier' effect appeared in February 1974, when later campaign polls consistently *overestimated* Liberal support.

Another way in which opinion poll results might influence voting has come to prominence in recent years. This is the role that polls can have in assisting tactical voting. A particularly striking example of this occurred in a by-election in Bermondsey, in February 1983. This had formerly been a very safe Labour seat but the Labour candidate in the by-election was highly unpopular and a majority of the electorate did not want to vote for him. There were, however, two other candidates in a position to challenge for the seat — an Alliance candidate and a local 'Real Labour' candidate. On the Friday before the election, an NOP poll was published in the *Daily Mail* showing support for the parties as Labour 37 per cent, Alliance 25 per cent, Real Labour 24 per cent and Conservative 11 per cent. Despite the statistical insignificance of the difference between the Alliance and Real Labour, the poll was widely interpreted as showing that the Alliance was in second place. On the following Tuesday, Thames Television announced the results of a poll by Opinion Research Centre which showed Labour and the Alliance neck-and-neck at 30 per cent each, followed by Real Labour on 16 per cent and the Conservatives on 10 per cent. These results were 'splashed' in the popular press. The election took place on the Thursday and the result was Alliance 58 per cent, Labour 26 per cent, Real Labour 8 per cent and Conservative 6 per cent. The most striking development in voting intentions during this by-election was the massive shift from Real Labour and the Conservatives to the Alliance, and it was widely claimed that the publication of the poll results decisively influenced the eventual outcome.

It is important to note, however, that this example concerns polls in a single constituency at a by-election. Since tactical voting is essentially a constituency-level matter, there is no straightforward way in which it could be based on nation-wide polls in a general election. Moreover, no constituency in a general election is the subject of the intense publicity and campaign activity that occurs in by-elections and there are relatively few single-constituency polls. Even when these are undertaken, their impact is much smaller. There is no evidence that the single-constituency polls that were published during recent general election campaigns had any systematic and significant impact on the results. Even in the Bermondsey case it is not clear that we should talk of the polls 'influencing' voters. Rather, it might be claimed that the polls merely provided neutral information of which voters could take account, if they so wished, in order to use their vote more effectively to achieve their desired outcome.

There is, then, little 'hard' evidence that public opinion polls directly influence voters in general elections. This is not to say that they are not an important aspect of election campaigns. Prime ministers use them to help decide on an election date; the political parties closely monitor public polls and themselves employ firms to do private polls on their behalf. The parties build their campaign strategies around what the polls tell them. The media also frequently use poll results as the centrepiece of their election coverage. During the 1992 campaign, for example, the reports of what the polls were saying constituted 18 per cent of front-page lead stories on the election in daily newspapers (Butler and Kavanagh, 1992, p. 201). Given their failure in 1992, it might be that the polls will not be so prominent in future elections but, in any event, the higher profile of polls in recent campaigns should not be confused with their ability to influence voters.

It is often argued that the publication of opinion poll results should be banned during election campaigns in Britain, as it is in some other countries. The Speaker's Conference on Electoral Reform recommended this in 1967 but the proposal was not accepted by the government. None the less, the issue continues to be raised. Those who favour banning them believe that polls do affect voting behaviour, and also argue that they 'trivialise' elections by reducing them to 'horse-races' and deflecting the attention of the voters from the serious issues at stake (see Whiteley, 1986).

If the publication of polls were banned, however, they would merely be replaced by leaks from private polls, rumour and deliberate disinformation campaigns. Local parties and candidates are not above referring to 'polls' of doubtful validity, or even inventing 'poll' results in their campaign literature. We are all familiar with the campaign organiser who claims that canvass returns show that his party is doing 'very well' and support is 'holding up', when the election result turns out to be a disaster. It seems better, on the whole, to have polls conducted by firms with no political axe to grind.

More positively, reliable information about the relative support for parties is something that voters may wish to take into account before deciding how to vote. And why should they be denied it?

Opinion polls by reputable companies can be counted as a benefit to the electoral process, not as a problem.

Conclusion

As compared with the 1950s and 1960s, election campaigns are now, potentially, more likely to influence voters and election outcomes. The same is true of the personalities of party leaders. The dealigned electorate is more open to change in the short term. If a party has a disastrous campaign or commits serious gaffes, or if a party leader is viewed as unsuitable, then the election result will be affected. If, however, all parties run careful, professional campaigns and there is not a great deal to choose between their leaders, then the short-term instability among the voters will not be markedly to the benefit or disadvantage of any one of them. It is important for a party to have good campaigns, however. The apparent lack of change among the electorate in 1987 and 1992 is deceptive — as any party that did not campaign seriously and well would soon find out.

Notes

1. The quotation is used as the title of an article on the 1987 campaign by Pippa Norris (1987). The allusion is, of course, to *Macbeth*, Act V Scene v.
2. This terminology is suggested by Norris (1987).
3. *The Times*, 24 March 1992.
4. The other adjustments included 'handsetting' seats. That is to say, there was a belief that in certain seats — those that had changed hands in a by-election and some where a strong SNP challenge was expected, for example — a national poll could not give an accurate prediction and so a subjective judgement about the likely outcome in these seats was made.

6

TRENDS IN GENERAL ELECTION RESULTS

In previous chapters I have been mainly concerned with survey evidence about voting behaviour in Britain. The focus has been on individual electors. In this chapter I consider election results themselves — the aggregate, net effect of the voting decisions made by individuals. There is an obvious link between individual behaviour and election results and we would expect the developments in voting behaviour at the individual level, which have been outlined in previous chapters, to be reflected at the aggregate level.

The study of election results has a lengthy tradition in Britain, predating the emergence of survey studies. After every election since 1945 a volume has been published (*The British General Election of . . .*), providing an account of the election campaign and analysis of the results. The books are known as the 'Nuffield studies' because of their connection with Nuffield College, Oxford, and, except for the first two, every one has been authored or co-authored by David Butler.

Any election contested by political parties provides two pieces of information which constitute the basic dependent variables in the analysis of election results — the number of eligible electors who vote (turn-out) and the distribution of votes among the competing parties. (Other information such as the number of spoiled ballot papers, the sex of candidates and the position of candidates on the ballot paper can also usually be obtained and used in analysis.) In a single general election, we have this information for all constituencies and we can analyse variations in the dependent variables across constituencies.[1] This is called *cross-sectional* analysis. When more than one election or a series is studied, we can also analyse change in the variables from one election to another. This is sometimes called *longitudinal* or *time-series* analysis.

Turn-out

Turn-out in British general elections varies both over time and across constituencies. The national turn-out since 1950 is shown in Table 6.1. The figures appear to indicate a downward trend until 1970 but this is rather misleading. The turn-outs in 1950 and 1951 were quite exceptional — from 1922 to 1945 the average turn-out was 74 per cent — and if these two are omitted, any downward trend is very slight indeed. Moreover, the figures are not directly comparable over the period. In 1970 the voting age was lowered from 21 to 18 and this increased the total electorate by more than three million as compared with 1966.

In an international context, it is worth noting that British turn-out is not particularly high. In a comparative study of turn-out, Crewe reports that Britain comes fourteenth out of twenty democracies in terms of turn-out in the post-war period (see Crewe, 1981b, pp. 234–6). Even so, it can be argued that turn-out in Britain is surprisingly high. Since most seats are 'safe' for one party or another, most electors know who is going to win their seat before they go to vote. In some respects voting is clearly an irrational act.

Table 6.1 Turn-out in general elections, 1950–92 (%).

1950	84.0	1970	72.0
1951	82.5	Feb. 1974	78.1
1955	76.8	Oct. 1974	72.8
1959	78.7	1979	76.0
1964	77.1	1983	72.7
1966	75.8	1987	75.3
		1992	77.7

Source: Butler and Kavanagh (1992, pp. 284–5).

It involves the individual voter in some costs — getting to the polls, for example — and the benefits are not obvious. The chances of an individual's vote making any difference to a constituency result, let alone the result of the election as a whole, are infinitesimal. None the less, most electors do turn out in general elections. Voting is widely believed to be a duty of citizens, and the costs involved are so small that they do not deter on the scale that 'pure' rational choice theory would predict (see McLean, 1982, ch. 4).

The comparative point made above raises an important question. What exactly do turn-out figures measure? Different countries have different rules about voting — in Australia it is compulsory, for example — and this affects the interpretation of the figures. In Britain, what is measured is the percentage of people whose names are on the electoral register who put a ballot paper into the ballot box. Compiling the electoral register is the responsibility of local authorities. The list is drawn up every October, usually on the basis of information supplied to the local authority on forms that are distributed to every household, institution or other place where voters might live. Although it is drawn up in October, the register does not come into force until the following February and then it lasts for one year.

Even when it is first compiled the register cannot possibly be 100 per cent accurate. People are accidentally missed off (most commonly young people who will become 18 before the register lapses); others are included who should not be; and yet others are registered in two places (students, for example, are often registered at their homes and at their college or university). When it comes into force the register is already four months out of date — people will have died, moved or emigrated — and it continues to decay during the year for which it is in force. Official turn-out figures do not take account of the accuracy of the electoral register but some electoral analysts have done. Rose (1974, p. 494), for example, calculates that the 'real' turn-out figure is obtained by the following formula:

$$\frac{\text{Reported percentage turn-out}}{(100 + 3.4 - 1.0 - 0.15m - 0.67m)}$$

In this formula, 'm' is the number of months from the compilation of the register to the election; 3.4 is added and 1.0 deducted to take

Table 6.2 Adjusted turn-out in general elections, 1950–92 (%).

1950	84.1	1970	75.2
1951	88.3	Feb. 1974	78.8
1955	79.8	Oct. 1974	78.6
1959	85.0	1979	78.6
1964 ·	83.3	1983	75.8
1966	77.4	1987	78.6
		1992	79.7

Note: Adjustments are made according to the formula described in the text.

account of citizens not registered and electors registered twice respectively; subtracting 0.15m and 0.67m adjusts for electors who have died and those who have moved.

National turn-out trends taking account of these adjustments are shown in Table 6.2. The impression given by these data is not one of a gentle decline but of a fairly sharp break between 1964 and 1966. Up to 1964, turn-out was well over 80 per cent in four out of five elections (and the fifth was very close to 80 per cent). From 1966 onwards (and that was before 18-year-olds were given the vote), turn-out has never exceeded 80 per cent but has regularly been in the mid-to-high seventies.

Turn-out variation from constituency to constituency is very large. In the 1992 election it ranged from 86.1 per cent (Leicestershire North West) to 53.9 per cent (Peckham). Excluding Northern Ireland, turn-out was less than 70 per cent in fifty-nine seats, while in sixty-eight seats it was 83 per cent or greater. Clearly, variations such as this require explanation and investigations of the topic have drawn attention to four main sorts of explanatory factor — 'practical', social, political and what, for want of a better term, might be called 'cultural'. The normal method of analysis used to investigate the problem is to try to explain the variation in the dependent variable (constituency turn-out) by reference to a series of independent variables, employing correlation and regression techniques.

An example of a simple practical matter affecting constituency turn-outs occurred at the 1992 election. The election took place during a university vacation and, since most students had returned home, constituencies with large resident student populations recorded turn-outs that were much lower than usual. In general, however, practical considerations relate to the accuracy of the electoral registers upon which turn-out calculations are based. If the registers in some constituencies are more inaccurate than in others, then they will appear to have lower turn-outs. Very low turn-outs tend to be found in inner-city constituencies. These also tend to be areas in which there are large floating populations and it seems likely that the low turn-out figures are in part a consequence of electoral register inaccuracy. Denver and Halfacree (1992a) tackle this problem more generally and find that the level of out-migration from a constituency has a significant negative effect on turn-out.

As an example of social influences upon constituency turn-out levels, Table 6.3 shows the correlations between eight indicators of the social composition of constituencies and turn-out at the 1983 election. The figures show, first, that there is a relationship between the occupational structure of constituencies and turn-out. More middle-class constituencies tend to have higher turn-outs and more working-class constituencies lower turn-outs. Housing tenure is also important. The correlation for percentage owner-occupiers is strongly positive while the other housing categories produce negative coefficients. High proportions of voters born in the New Commonwealth and Pakistan (a crude indicator of the proportion of ethnic minority voters) is associated with low levels of turn-out as is relatively large numbers of families without a car (which might be interpreted as a rough measure of poverty).

Table 6.3   Correlations between social composition and constituency turn-out in the 1983 election.

% professional and managerial workers	0.327
% working class	–0.234
% owner-occupiers	0.515
% council tenants	–0.335
% private tenants	–0.367
% born in New Commonwealth and Pakistan	–0.506
% households with no car	–0.632
% employed in agriculture	0.310

Note: The social composition variables derive from the 1981 census and the analysis is based on the 633 constituencies in Britain (excluding Northern Ireland).

Finally, the more people employed in agriculture (a measure of how urban or rural a constituency is), the higher tends to be the turn-out.

It must be stressed that these correlations are derived from aggregate data. They refer to the characteristics of constituencies, not individuals. We cannot infer from them that owner-occupiers turn out in greater numbers than other people or that ethnic minority electors tend not to vote. Rather the figures tell us that the greater the proportion of owner-occupiers in a constituency, the higher, usually, is the turn-out, and the more ethnic minority voters there are, the lower is the turn-out.

Correlations between turn-out and two 'political' factors are shown in Table 6.4. It might be expected that multi-party contests would generate more interest among electors, especially when there is considerable support for a 'minor' party, and lead to higher levels of turn-out. This was, indeed, the case up to 1979 — the coefficients are positive and statistically significant, although the strength of the relationship is somewhat erratic. In the 1980s and 1990s, however, candidacies by third and fourth parties became much more common and they ceased to have any effect on constituency turn-outs.

The other 'political' variable shown is the 'marginality', or the closeness of the contest, in the previous election. This has commonly been found to be an important predictor of constituency turn-out (see Denver and Hands, 1974, 1985; Eagles and Erfle, 1989; Lutz, 1991; Denver and Halfacree, 1992a). Even when a variety of other social and political variables was taken into account, marginality remained important. In an early analysis of this

Table 6.4 Correlations between minor-party support, marginality and turn-out, 1964–92.

	1964	1966	1970	Oct. 1974	1979	1983	1987	1992
% minor party	0.31	0.27	0.37	0.29	0.18	−0.09	−0.02	−0.04
Marginality	0.23	0.46	0.44	0.48	0.51	0.27	0.16	−0.05

Note: 'Minor party' support is the percentage voting for parties other than those that came first and second in the constituency concerned.

Source: The figures for 1964 to 1979 are from Denver and Hands (1985, pp. 382–4); those for 1983, 1987 and 1992 are original calculations.

topic, Denver and Hands (1974) inclined to the view that the effect of marginality was not a consequence of electors' calculating that it was more vital to vote in more marginal seats, but was a result of the fact that the parties usually put a greater campaign effort into more marginal seats. They later argued that things had changed in the 1970s, and that the increasingly strong correlations between marginality and turn-out reflected the fact that 'voters respond less to the stimulus of the party campaigns, and more to their own independent assessments of the likelihood of seats changing hands' (1985, p. 387). Denver and Hands confidently expected that the relationship between marginality and turn-out would continue to strengthen but, as the table shows, it became markedly weaker in 1983 and 1987 and vanished altogether in 1992. Thus far no convincing explanation for this weakening impact of marginality has been offered.

As noted earlier, the standard method of analysing variations in constituency turn-out is to include different sorts of variables in multiple regression equations. In this way their relative and total impact can be examined. Thus Denver and Halfacree (1992a) can explain about two-thirds of the variation in 1983 turn-out by reference to the proportion of households with no car, the level of out-migration and the marginality of the seat. As this example shows, even when the effects of mechanical, social and political influences are added together there still remains a good deal of turn-out variation that is unexplained and it may be that this is a result of further, rather vague cultural factors which are difficult to measure empirically. This might account for the fact that seats in Wales and in former mining areas have higher turn-outs than would be expected, for example. Similarly, the lower-than-expected turn-out in English inner cities may reflect local traditions or cultural norms, in addition to inaccurate registers and high levels of deprivation.

Studying voting as opposed to non-voting by means of surveys is not easy. Most people do vote in general elections and it is regularly found in surveys that some of those who have not voted, claim to have done so.[2] As a result, surveys often have relatively few genuine non-voters among their respondents and this inhibits analysis. To date, there have been two substantial considerations of non-voting at the individual level (Crewe, Fox and Alt, 1977; Swaddle and Heath, 1989).

Crewe *et al.* used BES survey data from the four general elections between 1966 and October 1974. They find, first of all, that very few people are consistent non-voters. If someone fails to vote in one election, he or she is quite likely to vote in the one after or the one after that. This is linked to the reasons for failing to vote, which are overwhelmingly 'accidental' or 'apathetic'. People may be away on polling day, or ill, or simply forget to vote. Very few are deliberate abstainers in the sense of refusing to vote on principle.

Crewe *et al.* also investigated the effects of a series of social variables on propensity to vote and find that most seem to have little effect. Working class people are as likely to vote as middle-class people, women as likely as men, the poorly educated as likely as the highly educated, and so on. Only four factors seem to be associated with poor turn-out: being young, single, living in privately rented accommodation and being residentially mobile. These are clearly strongly interconnected and they all involve isolation from social pressure, characteristic of stable communities, to conform to the norm of voting. The archetypal non-voter is a single young person who has recently moved into a bed-sit in South Kensington.

In a novel piece of analysis, Swaddle and Heath combine the 1987 BES survey data with detailed information from the electoral registers used by polling officials to mark off the names of people as they actually voted in the 1987 election. They are, therefore, able to analyse the characteristics of 'genuine', as opposed to 'admitted', non-voters. Their results almost entirely confirm those reported by Crewe and his colleagues. The one exception is that Swaddle and Heath find that class variables are related to propensity to vote — manual workers are less likely to vote than non-manual workers — although the relationship is not a strong one.

The most important political variable affecting the individual voter's propensity to turn out in elections is strength of party identification. This is consistently found in studies of electoral participation. Butler and Stokes (1974, p. 40) found in the early 1960s that 64 per cent of very strong identifiers voted in local elections, compared with 54 per cent of fairly strong identifiers and 39 per cent of not very strong identifiers. Figures from the analysis by Crewe and his colleagues, together with the 'official' turn-out of 1992 BES respondents, are given in Table 6.5, and the pattern is very clear.

Table 6.5   Turn-out by strength of party identification (%).

	Very strong	Fairly strong	Not very strong	No party identification
Regular voters (1966–74)	84	74	54	–
Voted 1992	92	90	80	58

Note: The first row shows the percentages who voted in all four general elections from 1966 to October 1974.
Source: Crewe, Fox and Alt (1977); BES 1992 cross-section survey.

The importance of party identification strength suggests an interpretation of the trend in overall aggregate turn-out which was reported in Table 6.2. Turn-out, it might be argued, was higher in the 1950s and 1960s because there were more strong identifiers in the electorate then. As the strength of party identification decreased thereafter, turn-out settled at a lower level. This is, of course, far from a full explanation of the trend in turn-out and the decline in party identification offers few clues about how to account for cross-sectional variation. But the generally lower level of national turn-out from 1966 onwards may be a consequence of partisan dealignment that is easily overlooked.

Patterns of party support 1950–70

In Chapter 2, I described the period 1950 to 1970 as, electorally, a period of alignment. Surveys revealed that voters were mainly influenced by long-term factors. They were aligned with the Conservative or Labour party and their vote was stable from election to election. To what extent is this mirrored in election results?

The distribution of votes at each election between 1950 and 1970 is given in Table 6.6 and the figures demonstrate, first, the electoral dominance of the two major parties. Their combined share of the votes averaged 91.8 per cent in these elections. (In terms of seats, two-party dominance was even greater, with an average of 98.5 per cent of seats won by the two parties.) Not surprisingly, the two parties monopolised government with Labour holding office during 1950–51 and 1964–70 and the Conservatives being in power from 1951 to 1964.

Table 6.6   National distribution of votes, 1950–70 (%).

	1950	1951	1955	1959	1964	1966	1970
Conservative	43.5	48.0	49.7	49.4	43.4	41.9	46.4
Labour	46.1	48.8	46.4	43.8	44.1	47.9	43.0
Liberal	9.1	2.5	2.7	5.9	11.2	8.5	7.5
Others	1.3	0.7	1.1	1.0	1.3	1.6	3.1
Overall swing	–	+0.9	+2.9	+1.2	–3.2	–2.7	+4.7

Source: Butler and Kavanagh (1992, pp. 284–5).

Second, the relative stability of support for the two major parties is also impressive. Over the twenty years, neither reached 50 per cent of the votes cast and neither fell below 40 per cent. Liberal support was rather more variable but this was largely due to variations in the number of Liberal candidates. The sharp rise in the votes obtained by 'others' in 1970 reflects the increased support obtained by the nationalist parties in Scotland and Wales at that election.

There was, of course, some change in support for the major parties from election to election. As measured by overall swing,[3] however, such changes tended to be small, with the exception of 1970 which was in many ways a watershed election. As I noted in Chapter 1, swing is a measure of net change in elections and it is likely that there was more individual change than the gross figures imply. None the less, the election results from 1950 to 1970 are very much what would be expected on the basis of the model of individual voting outlined in Chapter 2. Partisan and class alignment among voters sustained a stable two-party system at aggregate level.

One further feature of general election results in this period should be noted. Changes in the distribution of votes from one election to the next were remarkably uniform over the country as a whole. As Crewe puts it:

> In every election but one (1959) at least three-quarters of the constituency swings were within 2 per cent of the national median and only a handful of seats bucked the national trend. To know the swing in Cornwall was to know, within a percentage point or two, the swing in the Highlands; to know the results of the first three constituencies to declare on election night was to know not only which party had won — but by how many seats. (1985a, pp. 101–3)

The last point is something of an exaggeration but it is a pardonable one. Significant deviations from the national trend were relatively rare.

Exactly why swing in British elections was so uniform in this period is something of a mystery. A common-sense explanation might suggest that uniform swing was produced by uniform behaviour. Over the country as a whole, we might think, voters responded in the same way to national issues and events that were transmitted by national media during a national election campaign. But in this case common sense would be wrong. If, say, in every constituency 5 per cent of Labour voters in one election switched to the Conservatives at the next, this would not produce the same swing figure in every constituency. The reason is that 5 per cent of Labour voters in a safe Labour seat represents many more people than 5 per cent of Labour voters in a safe Conservative seat. In a safe Labour seat, therefore, a switch of this kind would have a far greater effect on the share of votes obtained by the parties than in a safe Conservative seat with only a small number of Labour voters in the first place. Consequently, the swing figures would be different.[4]

Butler and Stokes (1974, pp. 140–51) directly addressed the problem of uniform swing and suggested that it could be explained by the fact that, in any individual constituency, voters are influenced by both national and local forces. They argued that the influence of the local environment dampened or accentuated national movements and that these forces balanced out in such a way that swings ended up being of a similar size in different constituencies. It remains very difficult to explain, however, why relatively uniform swing should result from these processes.

Although uniform swing between pairs of elections was the rule between 1950 and 1970, there were two distinct cumulative trends in swing which began in the 1959 election. In the first place, in every election from 1959 to 1970 there was a tendency for constituencies in more urban areas to swing more heavily than average to Labour when the national trend was in Labour's favour, and less heavily than average to the Conservatives (or even in the opposite direction) when the national swing was to the Conservatives. In more rural seats the opposite was the case. Second, there were similar cumulative movements towards Labour in Scotland and the

Table 6.7 Correlations between socioeconomic characteristics of English constituencies and party shares of votes, 1970.

	% Con.	% Lab.		% Con.	% Lab.
% non-manual	0.59	−0.60	% young voters	0.03	0.02
% manual	−0.31	0.38	% aged 65+	0.42	−0.49
% owner-occupiers	0.53	−0.55	% female	0.30	−0.29
% council tenants	−0.37	0.42	% born in New Commonwealth	−0.06	0.12

Source: Crewe and Payne (1971, p. 419).

North of England, and towards the Conservatives in the South of England and the Midlands. These trends became even more pronounced after 1970 and had important consequences for the operation of the electoral system which I consider below.

Until the late 1960s, the analysis of aggregate election statistics was normally confined to the election results themselves (as in the statistical appendices to the Nuffield studies). There were very few examples of analysis that attempted to relate the distribution of party support in constituencies to their socioeconomic characteristics in a systematic way. The reason for this was that it was not until the sample census of 1966 that census data were made available on a constituency basis. In the Nuffield study of the 1970 election, however, Ivor Crewe and Clive Payne (1971) demonstrated the possibilities for aggregate analysis that had been opened up by the availability of census data for constituencies. Among other things, they calculated the correlations between a variety of socioeconomic factors and party shares of the vote, and a selection of these is reproduced in Table 6.7.

The occupational class composition of constituencies (per cent non-manual) produced the best single correlation with party support, although the class-related housing variables (per cent owner-occupiers, per cent council tenants) also correlated well. The apparent absence of a relationship between major-party support on the one hand, and the percentages of young voters and of those born in the New Commonwealth on the other, is a useful reminder of the pitfalls of inferring individual behaviour from aggregate statistics. We know from survey data that, as a matter of fact, both of these groups disproportionately supported

Labour. In most constituencies, however, they constituted such a small fraction of the electorate that variations in their size had no impact on the votes received by the parties, and hence the correlations are weak.

A more exhaustive analysis of the social correlates of constituency voting patterns in the 1966 general election was undertaken by Miller (1977). Miller examined the effect of forty-two socioeconomic variables upon levels of party support and found that 'when the census variables were used to predict Labour versus Conservative votes in the constituencies, the occupation variables were by far the most effective' (p. 27). Easily the most important single predictor variable was the percentage of employers and managers in a constituency, which had a correlation of 0.71 with per cent Conservative and –0.84 with per cent Labour. The class character of a constituency was, then, the best guide to its political character.

In general terms, the results of these sorts of analyses were not exactly news to any observer of British electoral politics. Most people knew that middle-class areas usually returned Conservative MPs and that working-class areas voted Labour. However, aggregate data analysis, at the least, brought a new precision to knowledge of this kind. Correlation coefficients enabled researchers to tell exactly how strongly certain characteristics of constituencies were related to levels of party support; regression equations clarified the nature of such relationships and enabled analysts to identify constituencies in which the pattern of party support deviated from what would be expected on the basis of their social composition. The availability of appropriate data allowed more subtle and sophisticated analysis of election results than had hitherto been possible.

Examination of aggregate voting patterns from 1950 to 1970, then, seems to fulfil the expectations that we would have on the basis of the discussion of individual voting behaviour in Chapter 2. The two major parties dominated elections, their support was stable, inter-election change was relatively small and variations in constituency voting patterns were best explained by variations in class composition. I have suggested in earlier chapters, however, that there were major changes in voting behaviour after 1970 and we must now consider the extent to which these are reflected in aggregate patterns.

Patterns of party support 1970–87

After 1970 survey studies suggested that voters were increasingly dealigned. They were not as strongly committed to the major parties as before and the connections between class and party support became weaker. Voters were more volatile and more influenced by short-term electoral forces. Given this, we might expect that election results would show more volatility. With the stabilising influence of class and party identification reduced, change rather than stability is to be expected. It is not, however, quite as straightforward as this. It is possible, for instance, that short-term forces could favour the same party in successive elections, or that increased volatility at the individual level could be self-cancelling. In these cases the election results would give the appearance of stability. The absence of sharp swings in elections cannot in itself, then, be taken as a refutation of the dealignment thesis. On the other hand, sharp net changes in at least some elections would constitute strong evidence of a more dealigned electorate.

The shares of votes received by the parties in general elections from 1970 to 1987 are shown in Table 6.8. Clearly, the two major parties experienced a sharp decline in popularity during this period. Their combined support had averaged 91.8 per cent of the vote in the seven elections to 1970 but only 74.8 per cent in the five elections after that. Neither the Conservatives nor Labour reached the level of support that they had *averaged* between 1950 and 1970 in a single election thereafter. This electoral decline was not reflected in the House of Commons where the two parties continued to dominate, with only a slightly reduced average of 93.9 per cent

Table 6.8 National distribution of votes, 1974–92 (%).

	Feb. 1974	Oct. 1974	1979	1983	1987	1992
Conservative	37.8	35.8	43.9	42.4	42.3	41.9
Labour	37.1	39.2	37.0	27.6	30.8	34.4
Liberal, etc.	19.3	18.3	13.8	25.4	22.6	17.8
Others	5.8	6.7	5.3	4.6	4.3	5.8
Overall swing	–1.4	–2.1	+5.2	+4.0	–1.7	–2.0

Source: Butler and Kavanagh (1992, pp. 284–5).

of seats won. But even this small reduction made it more difficult for one party to gain an overall majority of seats: in the second half of the 1970s the Labour government lost its majority and had to rely on the support of Liberals and others to stay in office.

Support for the two parties was also more variable than before. The Conservative share of votes fell by more than ten points between 1970 and October 1974 before recovering to stabilise at just over 40 per cent from 1979 onwards. Labour, on the other hand, has not achieved 40 per cent in a general election since 1970 and in the 1983 election recorded its lowest vote share since 1918, more than 15 points below its 1970 level.

The other side of the coin to reduced major-party support is, of course, increased support for what may for convenience be termed the centre — the Liberals from 1974 to 1979, the Alliance (SDP and Liberals) in 1983 and 1987 and the Liberal Democrats in 1992. The Liberals by themselves achieved a remarkable leap of almost 12 points between 1970 and February 1974 but fell away somewhat after that. In 1981, however, a new party — the SDP — was formed as a breakaway from Labour. The fact that a new party could be formed and immediately attract high levels of public support is itself an indicator of the fluid nature of party loyalties at this time. The SDP and the Liberals fought the 1983 and 1987 elections together as the Alliance, and their share of the vote in 1983 was the highest 'third party' vote since 1923. In 1992, however, the Liberal Democrats (formed by a merger between the Liberals and the SDP) polled less well than the Liberals alone had in 1974.

The higher level of support for 'others' after 1970, which the table shows, is in part simply a reflection of a change in the way in which votes cast in Northern Ireland are now categorised.[5] But it also reflects more nationalist voting in Scotland and Wales as well as increased support for Greens and others.

Despite the increased variability in major-party support after 1970, the figures for swing shown in Table 6.8 are not very remarkable. It is true that the 5.2 per cent swing recorded in 1979 was the largest since the war and the 1983 swing was also higher than the post-war average. But the other four swings were relatively small. This might appear to contradict the claim that variability in levels of party support increased during this period. But swing is a measure of the relative changes in support for the two major parties only; it does not directly take account of the performances of other parties.

Table 6.9 Pedersen index scores, 1951–92.

1951	7.7	Feb. 1974	14.5
1955	2.4	Oct. 1974	3.0
1959	3.1	1979	8.1
1964	6.0	1983	11.6
1966	4.2	1987	3.2
1970	6.0	1992	5.2

A measure of net electoral change which does do this is the Pedersen index (named after its inventor, Mogens Pedersen, a Danish political scientist). This index is created by adding together the percentage point change in *all* parties' shares of the vote between two elections and dividing the result by two. Thus, from Table 6.8 the changes between 1987 and 1992 were 0.4 (Conservative), 3.6 (Labour), 4.8 (Liberal Democrats) and 1.5 (others). These sum to 10.3, so the index score is 5.2.

Table 6.9 shows the index score for post-war elections. Overall, the scores after 1970 average 7.6 compared with 4.9 before. Two post-1970 elections have low scores (October 1974, which followed very shortly after the previous election, and 1987). As I explained above, however, these indications of low aggregate volatility do not, in themselves, contradict the argument that individual voting was more dealigned. On the other hand, the very high scores in February 1974, 1979 and 1983, and the fairly high score in 1992, are clear reflections at aggregate level of dealignment at the level of individual voters.

Changes in party support in individual constituencies after 1970 have been characterised by an increase in variability. The days of a nationally uniform swing have gone. As I indicated in Chapter 1, the spread or dispersion of a set of scores is measured by a statistic called the standard deviation, and the standard deviations of constituency swings in elections since 1959 are shown in Table 6.10. The standard deviations were fairly constant until 1979 but since then have been larger, indicating greater variability in swing from constituency to constituency. The distance we have travelled, as it were, from uniform swing can be illustrated by the fact that in the 1992 election the pattern of change from 1987 implied by the national trend (falls in the Conservative and Liberal Democrat vote shares and a rise in the Labour vote) occurred in just over half (334) of constituencies.

Table 6.10   Standard deviation of two-party swings, 1959–92.

1959	1964	1966	1970	Oct. 1974	1979	1983	1987	1992
2.7	3.1	2.1	2.6	2.4	4.1	5.1	4.1	4.1

Note: The election of February 1974 is omitted because there were major constituency boundary changes and (unlike in 1983) there are no reliable estimates of what the result of the previous election would have been in the new constituencies.
Sources: Curtice and Steed (1980, p. 394; 1984, p. 334; 1988, p. 317; 1992, p. 323).

It is not easy to convey the meaning and the extent of the increased variability of swing in figures. The standard deviation is not an easy statistic to interpret. However, a visual impression of what the increasing standard deviation of swing means is given in Figure 6.1, which shows the approximate distribution of constituencies around the mean swing in 1966 and 1987. In 1966, most constituencies were closely bunched around the mean. The graph

Table 6.11   Long-term deviations in two-party swing.

	Total 1955–70	1970–87	1955–87
South of England	+1.7	+7.2	+8.9
Midlands	+3.1	+2.8	+5.9
North of England	–2.0	–7.0	–9.0
Scotland	–4.8	–14.3	–19.1
Wales	–1.9	+3.5	+0.6
	1955–70	1970–79	1955–79
City	–3.9	–4.5	–8.4
Very urban	–2.8	–2.8	–5.6
Mainly urban	–0.1	–0.8	–0.9
Mixed	+1.4	+2.0	+3.4
Mainly rural	+3.2	+3.8	+7.0
Very rural	+2.7	+6.0	+8.7

Notes: Each entry is the difference between the mean two-party swing in the category of constituency concerned and the mean for all constituencies. A plus sign indicates a deviation in favour of the Conservatives and a minus sign a deviation in favour of Labour. The trend of urban–rural deviation continued in 1983 but Curtice and Steed used a different categorisation from that used previously and their analysis of the 1987 election does not contain comparable data.
Sources: Curtice and Steed (1986, p.212; 1988, p.330).

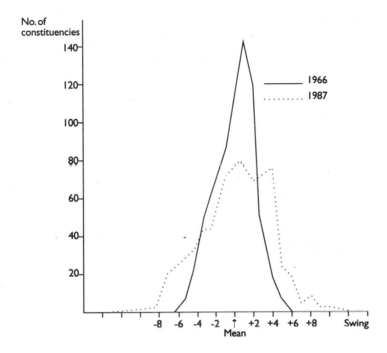

Figure 6.1 Distribution of two-party swing across constituencies, 1966 and 1987.

for 1987 is much flatter and more spread out. It is this difference that the relevant standard deviation statistics indicate.

Increased variation in constituency swings has been partly caused by a continuation and acceleration of the deviating trends that began in 1959. In every election until 1987, whatever its direction on national figures, swing deviated towards Labour in the North of England, Scotland and more urban seats, whereas in the Midlands, the South and more rural areas it deviated towards the Conservatives. The cumulative effects of regional deviations between 1955 and 1987 and of urban-rural differences between 1955 and 1979 are summarised in Table 6.11. The pattern here is remarkably regular with both regional and urban–rural deviations from the national trend becoming more marked, on the whole after 1970.

When regional and urban–rural categories are combined, the long-term cumulative divergences in swing are truly enormous. At the extremes, between 1955 and 1979 the swing in very rural constituencies in the Midlands and South of England deviated from the national figure by a total of 12.3 points towards the Conservatives, while cities in Scotland deviated by 19.1 points towards Labour. Over the country as a whole, there was a swing of 1.8 per cent towards the Conservatives between 1955 and 1979, but rural areas in the South and Midlands had a 14.1 per cent swing to the Conservatives and Scottish cities swung 17.3 per cent to Labour. Curtice and Steed do not give exactly comparable figures for the 1983 election but the pattern of previous elections was repeated, with swings ranging from 11.0 per cent to the Conservatives in the rural Midlands to 2.5 per cent to Labour in urban Scotland (Curtice and Steed, 1984, p. 338). In the 1987 election, however, although the familiar regional deviations appeared yet again, the long-term trend in respect of urban and rural areas came to an end and there was no marked urban–rural divergence in terms of swing.

The cumulative effect of regional deviations was such that by the 1980s Labour support was heavily concentrated in Scotland, Wales and the North while the Conservative vote was concentrated in the South. Talk of an electoral 'North–South divide' was common. Like most generalisations, the idea of an electoral dichotomy between the North and South of the country is an oversimplification, but it does highlight a major feature of the current pattern of party support in Britain.[6]

In Chapter 2, I briefly noted some explanations for regional divergence in elections up to 1970. The accentuation of regional differences after 1970 has focused more attention on the problem. Curtice and Steed (1982) suggest that there are three main explanations for the trend. First, there have been slow changes in the distribution of socioeconomic characteristics among the electorate. The proportion of broadly middle-class people has tended to increase in the South and in rural areas and, relatively speaking, to decrease in the North, Scotland and urban areas. It is worth noting, however, that recent research on the electoral effects of patterns of migration within Britain suggests that population movement has not contributed significantly to the growth of the regional and urban–rural divides (see Denver and Halfacree, 1992b; McMahon,

Heath, Harrop and Curtice, 1992). Second, differential regional behaviour, even within classes, is a product of regional variations in economic well-being. Put crudely, Scotland and the North are simply not as prosperous as the South. Third, there is a purely political explanation. As third parties have increased in popularity, this has generally been at the expense of the locally weaker major party. Since the Conservatives were already weaker in the North and Scotland, they suffered more from the increase in support for the Liberals, Alliance and SNP after 1970. They thus performed poorly relative to Labour and this is reflected in the swing figures. In the South, the picture is reversed, with Labour being the party to suffer.

The leading analysts of British electoral geography are Ron Johnston and Charles Pattie. With other colleagues they have produced a stream of books and articles detailing the nature and extent of the regional electoral divide and seeking to explain it (see, for example, Johnston, Pattie and Allsop, 1988; Pattie *et al.*, 1992; Pattie, Johnston and Fieldhouse, 1993). Although they show that different factors are involved, their main contention is that the growing regional electoral divide of the past thirty years or so is closely related to uneven regional economic development. Areas that have generally suffered economically have moved away from the Conservatives while those that have prospered have deserted Labour. They argue that recent government policy has had a differential regional impact, including changes in levels of unemployment, the occupational and industrial structure, and property values. Opinion poll data show that these have resulted in regional variations in satisfaction with the country's economic performance and in optimism about the economic future. In turn, this is reflected in divergences in regional voting patterns.

Given this interpretation, Johnston and Pattie would not have been surprised by the results of the 1992 election, which saw a reversal of the trend towards an ever-widening regional cleavage. Labour advanced more strongly in the Midlands and South than in the North of England and actually lost support in Scotland; the Conservatives lost most ground in the Midlands and South while improving their position slightly in Scotland and the North. As Pattie *et al.* (1993) demonstrate, these electoral patterns reflected the regional patterns of the 1988–92 economic recession. Whereas in previous recessions it had been the North of the country that suffered most, in this case the recession hit the Midlands and South earlier and harder than elsewhere.

Arguments in terms of uneven regional economic development are mainly directed to explaining changes in regional patterns of party support since 1955 (or even more recently), and they certainly shed a good deal of light on them. It is, however, still difficult to account for the very long-standing regional differences which have been clear since at least 1918. At root, as Curtice and Steed imply, these are likely to be a product of 'cultural or historical differences and defy economic interpretations' (1988, p. 333).

The long-term divergences in party support in Britain — both regionally and between urban and rural areas — have had important consequences for the operation of the electoral system. These are explored in detail by Curtice and Steed (1982, 1986). It used to be the case that the share of seats that a party would obtain in the House of Commons, on the basis of a given share of the total national vote, could be predicted fairly well by using the 'cube law'. If the share of votes between two parties were in the ratio A:B, then the share of seats would be in the ratio $A^3:B^3$. Thus, if the ratio of the two-party vote were 3:2, then the ratio of seats would be 27:8 ($3 \times 3 \times 3 : 2 \times 2 \times 2$). In other words, the party that obtained 60 per cent of the votes would get 77 per cent of the seats, while the other party with 40 per cent of the votes would get only 23 per cent of the seats. Clearly, then, the winning party's lead in terms of votes was greatly exaggerated by the electoral system when it was translated into seats.

The trends in support since 1955, however, have had the effect of making Labour seats more safely Labour and Conservative seats more safely Conservative. As a result, there have been fewer and fewer marginal seats. In 1955, 166 seats could be classed as marginal but by 1983 there were only 80 (Curtice and Steed, 1986, p. 214). There are now fewer seats for a party to gain for each percentage point swing in its favour, and fewer will be lost by incumbents for each point of swing against their party. Much bigger swings in votes are now required for the party in opposition to gain enough seats to achieve a majority in the House of Commons. The exaggerative quality of the electoral system has declined such that the ratio of seats to votes can no longer be predicted by a 'cube law' or even a 'square law'. Indeed, by the 1992 election the electoral system failed to produce any exaggerative effect at all.

The ratio of Conservative to Labour votes was 55:45 and the ratio of Conservative to Labour seats won was also 55:45 (see Curtice, 1992).

The publication of census data for parliamentary constituencies, which began in 1966, was continued for the censuses of 1971 and 1981. This has given rise to a flourishing industry in the aggregate analysis of election data.[7] It is impossible to summarise this extensive literature here so I will confine discussion to two important points.

The first centres on the data reproduced in Table 6.12 which shows the correlations between seven socioeconomic variables and the shares of votes received by the three leading parties in British constituencies in the 1987 general election. What these coefficients indicate is that by the late 1980s there was still a very strong relationship between the socioeconomic characteristics of a constituency and the level of its support for the Labour and Conservative parties. Indeed, the correlations here are stronger than the comparable figures given in Table 6.7 for the 1970 election. The correlations between Alliance support and these social characteristics, however, are only moderate. This is something that is generally true of support for third parties in Britain — it is always less strongly related to the socioeconomic characteristics of constituencies than is support for Labour or the Conservatives. Put another way, the level of third-party support in a constituency is less predictable than support for the other parties. This applies to the SNP, as well as to the Liberals, Alliance and Liberal Democrats. It is probably a function of the fact that these parties do not attempt to appeal directly to specific social groups. The relatively weak aggregate correlations for Alliance support — although they indicate some structuring by socioeconomic characteristics — tend to confirm survey findings that Alliance support in 1987 and Liberal Democrat support in 1992 was more evenly spread across social groups than was support for the major parties.

The second discussion point also arises directly out of the data in Table 6.12. I have argued that, at the individual level, voting behaviour in Britain after 1970 was characterised by a loosening of the relationship between social characteristics — especially social class — and party choice. Yet the table shows very strong correlations at aggregate level between the class make-up of constituencies (per cent employers and managers and per cent working

Table 6.12   Correlations between socioeconomic characteristics of constituencies and party shares of vote, 1987.

	% Conservative	% Labour	% Alliance
% employers and managers	0.78	–0.83	0.48
% working class	–0.77	0.82	–0.48
% with degree	0.41	–0.50	0.31
% car owners	0.74	–0.78	0.45
% owner-occupiers	0.68	–0.60	0.31
% council tenants	–0.72	0.68	–0.38
% unemployed	–0.73	0.75	–0.42

Source: Butler and Kavanagh (1988, p. 286).

class), and the level of support for the Conservatives and Labour. Indeed, these correlations are stronger for the 1987 election than they were in 1966 or 1970. This appears to contradict the thesis of class dealignment.

In fact, the discrepancy between aggregate and individual data is more apparent than real. The fact that per cent employers and managers correlates strongly with per cent Conservative means that the bigger the proportion of employers and managers in a constituency, the higher is the Conservative share of the vote. However, this might reflect the fact that the more employers and managers there are, the more *everyone*, irrespective of their class, votes Conservative. It tells us nothing about the extent of individual class voting.

In his work on this problem Miller (1977, 1978, 1979) has shown that the relationship between the class character of constituencies and their vote is stronger than would be expected on the basis of any given level of individual class voting. Where the Conservatives would be expected to do well on the basis of the class composition of the constituency, they do even better; where they would be expected to do badly, they do even worse. The same applies to Labour. Constituencies, in short, are more polarised politically than people. The correlations at aggregate level are stronger than the correlation at individual level. Once again this is compatible with individual dealignment. Indeed, if more and more working-class people vote Conservative in predominantly middle-class areas, and more and more middle-class people vote Labour in predominantly working-class areas, the effect would be to produce both increased polarisation at the constituency level and decreased class voting at the level of the individual voter.

The question remains, however, as to why the constituency effect occurs: why do people tend to follow locally dominant political norms irrespective of class? Miller's answer is a version of the 'neighbourhood' effect mentioned briefly in Chapter 2. The crucial feature of a voter's local environment is the concentration (or absence) of what Miller sees as 'core' classes. These are the 'controllers' (employers and managers) and 'anti-controllers' (manual workers who are trade union members). Concentrations of these classes set the tone, as it were, of an area and their influence is reinforced by personal contacts. As Miller puts it, 'Those who speak together vote together' (1977, p. 65). He concludes that 'the class characteristics of the social environment have more effect on constituency partisanship than class differences themselves . . . the partisanship of individuals is influenced more by where they live than what they do'. There is no conflict, then, between the aggregate data statistics shown in Table 6.12 and the general interpretation of trends in voting behaviour which I have advanced in previous chapters. The spatial polarisation of support for the two major parties has itself contributed to a damping down of the effect of traditional social cleavages.

The idea of a 'neighbourhood effect' has also been used to explain the regional differences discussed above. If the social context within which people live affects their choice of party then the fact that the social contexts of the North and the South are different in broad terms helps to account for their regional divergence. Rose and McAllister dissent from this view, arguing that if voters' family loyalties, socioeconomic characteristics and political values are taken into consideration, then 'where a voter lives is of very little relevance' (1990, p. 124). The point is, however, that voters' political values are themselves shaped by the kinds of area in which they live.

In an ingenious piece of analysis Harrop, Heath and Openshaw (1992) use census enumeration district data (enumeration districts typically contain about 190 households) to categorise the 'neighbourhoods' lived in by 1987 BES respondents. They find that there is indeed a very strong relationship between neighbourhood type and party choice. They then go on to investigate the various mechanisms by which this effect might operate — through political discussion between neighbours, party activity in the locality, and so on. Oddly, however, the only mechanism that their data support is self-selection of neighbourhoods. When people move house, they tend to move to areas that are predominantly of their own party colour. It is hard to believe that people weigh up the political complexion of an area to which they intend to move, and Harrop *et al.* suggest that it is an unintended consequence of other criteria. They conclude:

> In general these findings reflect the tenor of much research on contextual influences. A straightforward correlation between neighbourhood and voting shows evidence consistent with a neighbourhood effect, and this persists even when we control for a wide range of individual characteristics. When we look for the mechanisms of neighbourhood influence, however, we are less successful. (p. 118)

Conclusion

Before 1970, general election results were marked by two-party dominance and by stability. Aligned voting among individuals sustained a cohesive, class-based, stable two-party system. After 1970, dealignment increased and the party system became more fragmented. Elections were marked by instability and fluidity. In the final chapter I will look in more detail at the 1992 election, and speculate a little about how British electoral politics might develop in the next few years.

Notes

1. The total number of UK constituencies has been slowly increasing in the post-war period. In the elections of 1950 and 1951 there were 625, from 1955 to 1970 there were 630, from February 1974 to 1979 there were 635, from 1983 to 1987 there were 650 and in 1992 the total reached 651. In most analyses, constituencies in Northern Ireland (currently 17) are omitted.
2. By comparing official records with survey responses, Swaddle and Heath (1989) established that, among respondents to the 1987 BES survey who had not voted, about a quarter erroneously claimed to have voted in the election.

3. 'Overall' swing is calculated from the distribution of votes over the country as a whole. It should be distinguished from *mean* swing, which is the average of swings in all the individual constituencies.

4. For further explanation and discussion of this somewhat difficult point, see McLean (1973).

5. Until 1970 Ulster Unionist MPs took the Conservative party whip in the House of Commons, and Unionist votes were routinely added to the Conservative total. After 1970, however, the Unionist monolith fragmented (as did the traditional nationalist vote in the province) and Unionist MPs distanced themselves from the Conservatives. From February 1974 to 1987, normal practice was to treat all votes cast in Northern Ireland as 'others'. In 1992, however, there were eleven Conservative candidates in Northern Ireland.

6. The regional distribution of votes in the 1992 election is given in Table 7.2.

7. Constituency data from the 1991 census were not available at the time of writing. Since censuses are held only once every ten years, it is worth remembering that there is likely to be considerable inaccuracy when census data are used in conjunction with the results of an election that is distant in time from the date of the census.

7

THE 1992 GENERAL ELECTION AND THE ELECTORAL OUTLOOK

The 1992 election

The results of the 1992 general election were a great surprise to most people. Between 1987 and 1992 the Conservative record in local elections and by-elections had been dismal and their opinion poll ratings mediocre. The chances of the general election producing a 'hung' parliament — a situation in which no one party has a majority over all the others combined — appeared good. Even if their mid-term unpopularity could be put down to the normal inter-election cycle of government popularity, the Conservatives did not appear to have made the usual pre-election recovery and almost all opinion polls during the campaign indicated that they would lose their overall majority in the House of Commons. Exit polls on election day itself led the BBC and ITN to predict a hung parliament and, even when the results started to come in, television analysts and commentators appeared to take a long time to predict a Conservative victory. In the event, as Table 7.1 shows, the Conservatives all but retained their share of the vote and won an overall majority of 21 seats. Labour's share of the vote increased — but by less than expected — while that of the Liberal Democrats was almost five points lower than the Alliance achieved in 1987.

Table 7.1 General election result, 1992.

	Share of votes (%)	Change 1987–92	Seats	Change 1987–92
Conservative	41.9	–0.4	336	–40
Labour	34.4	+3.6	271	+42
Liberal Democrats	17.8	–4.8	20	–2
Others	5.8	+1.5	24	+1

Source: Butler and Kavanagh (1992, pp. 284–5).

It is not my intention here to discuss in detail what went wrong with the opinion polls in 1992 since that has already been done by others (see, for example, Butler and Kavanagh, 1992, ch. 7; Crewe, 1992d). Some of the explanations put forward concentrate on technical problems of sampling. It is suggested, for example, that the source that the pollsters rely on to determine the make-up of their sample in terms of class, housing tenure and so on (usually the 1981 census) is now out of date. It has also been suggested that the electoral register was more inaccurate than usual and that, in particular, the polls interviewed people — mostly Labour supporters — who had not registered to vote in order to try to avoid paying the poll tax. Another explanation, and one that would exonerate the pollsters, is that there was a very late swing of opinion towards the Conservatives — it is generally agreed that this accounted for the previous failure of the polls in 1970 — but analysts have found little evidence that there was a swing of the size and lateness required. Some of the more fruitful explanations concentrate on poll respondents. It has been suggested, first, that the sorts of people who refused to be interviewed were more likely to be Conservative supporters — older women, for example. But this has always been the case and leaves unanswered the question of what went so wrong in 1992. What was different in this case, it has been suggested, was that intending Conservatives believed that they would be thought selfish and uncaring if they owned up to supporting the government and therefore declined to be interviewed, or even misled interviewers as to their true intentions. This has been dubbed 'the shame factor'. Other Conservative supporters may have misled interviewers because they wanted to send a message of protest to the government, to express unhappiness at the way things were going. It is safe to do this in answer to poll questions but when it came to actually voting — when there was a distinct possibility that the government would be ousted — they drew back from the real consequences of voting against the government.

Clearly these last two suggestions are highly speculative but it is interesting to note that after the election one polling company (ICM) began to ask its respondents to indicate their voting intentions by marking a secret ballot paper, rather than answering a question, and has found that this produces higher Conservative and lower Labour figures than the conventional method.[1]

It is also not my intention in this chapter to provide a detailed analysis of the election results or an interpretation of why Labour lost and the Conservatives won. Analyses of the results have been provided by Curtice and Steed (1992) and Crewe, Norris and Waller (1992), while explanations of the outcome can be found in Sanders (1992) and Crewe (1992b), as well as in a plethora of newspaper articles. Rather, I first take some of the themes that I have discussed in previous chapters and consider what light is thrown on them by the 1992 election, and then go on to speculate briefly on the electoral outlook for the major parties.

Variations in swing

I suggested in Chapter 6 that in the 1970s inter-election change in individual constituencies became more variable. In 1992 the variation in constituency swings was again at the relatively high level seen in recent elections (see Table 6.10). In part the variation was regional — but on this occasion the thirty-year trend towards a North–South polarisation was reversed. As the figures for change in party support in Table 7.2 indicate, the Conservatives increased their share of the vote in Scotland, the North and Yorkshire and Humberside and lost most in the South, while Labour, on the whole, did better in the South than in Scotland and the North of England. Most commentators suggest that the reason for the reversal of the long-term regional trend was the uneven regional impact of the economic recession (see Pattie *et al.*, 1993) but the slight improvement in the position of the Conservatives in Scotland may also be explained by their efforts to rally pro-Union Scottish opinion behind them.

The reversal of the trend towards an increasing North–South electoral divide needs to be kept in perspective, however. It could hardly go on increasing indefinitely, since there must be a rock bottom below which a major party cannot fall even in the areas where it is most unpopular. As the first three columns of figures in Table 7.2 show, the North–South cleavage still exists. Support for the two major parties remains geographically concentrated and the decrease in North–South polarisation in 1992 was only slight. Despite all the post-election talk of the Conservatives' 'success' in Scotland, for example, they still ended up with only 25.7 per cent of the vote which was their second worst performance since 1945. The Conservatives gained more than 44 per cent of the vote in every region from the Midlands southwards, but had well under 40 per cent in northern England and less than 30 per cent in Wales and Scotland. Labour got more than 40 per cent in the three most northerly English regions and in Wales, but is still very weak in the South. In contrast, the Liberal Democrat vote is spread relatively evenly, with only Wales, Scotland and the South West deviating markedly from the overall average. The effect of these patterns of voting support for the parties is that party representation in the House of Commons remains geographically skewed. After the

Table 7.2   Regional variations in party support, 1992.

	% share of votes			Change 1987–92		
	Con.	Lab.	Lib. Dem.	Con.	Lab.	Lib. Dem.
Scotland	25.7	39.0	13.1	+1.6	–3.4	–6.1
Wales	28.6	49.5	12.4	–1.0	+4.4	–5.5
North	33.4	50.6	15.5	+1.0	+4.2	–5.5
Yorks./Humberside	37.9	44.4	16.8	+0.5	+3.7	–4.8
North West	37.8	44.9	15.8	–0.2	+3.7	–4.8
West Midlands	44.8	38.8	15.0	–0.8	+5.5	–5.8
East Midlands	46.6	37.4	15.2	–2.0	+7.4	–5.7
East Anglia	51.0	28.0	19.5	–1.1	+6.3	–6.2
South East	51.2	26.6	20.4	–1.0	+4.3	–4.5
South West	47.6	19.2	31.4	–3.0	+3.3	–1.6

Notes: Percentages do not total 100 because votes for other parties and candidates are not shown. In Scotland the SNP obtained 21.5% of the votes: a change of +7.4 on 1987. In Wales Plaid Cymru obtained 8.8% (+1.5).

Source: Butler and Kavanagh (1992, pp. 286–7).

1992 election, only 70 of the 336 Conservative MPs represented constituencies in Scotland, Wales or the North of England. On the other hand, 183 of the 271 Labour MPs came from these areas and only 88 came from the whole of the rest of England.

The other long-term geographical trend in party support which I noted in Chapter 6 was the tendency since 1959 for the ratio of Conservative to Labour support to increase in more rural areas and decrease in urban areas, especially large cities. In the 1987 election there was no significant difference in swing between urban and rural areas but in 1992 the tendency for them to diverge re-appeared. In very urban constituencies the Conservative-to-Labour swing was 3.1 per cent, in mainly urban areas it was 2.5 per cent, in mixed areas 2.2 per cent and in rural areas 1.9 per cent.

Another source of constituency variation in 1992 was tactical voting. Tactical voting occurs when someone does not vote for their most preferred party because it has no chance of winning but votes for their second preference, since this party is in closer con-tention with the party that the voter dislikes most. The extent of tactical voting is relevant to the main themes that I have discussed because it would be expected to be more common among a de-aligned, rather than an aligned, electorate (see Galbraith and Rae, 1989).

In their report on the 1987 election Heath *et al.* (1991, ch. 40) reported that 'only' 6.0 per cent of voters said that the main reason for their choice of party was tactical. Using a completely different methodology, Johnston and Pattie (1991) estimate that the figure was 7.7 per cent, which they interpret as 'a very substantial volume of tactical voting' (p. 104). Other analysts, using the same data as Heath *et al.* but utilising responses to additional questions, suggest that the proportion of tactical voters was 17 per cent overall and was higher among those who were better educated, had weak party identification or lived in a constituency where tactical voting made sense (see Niemi, Whitten and Franklin, 1992).

Heath *et al.* concede that the level of tactical voting has probably increased since the 1960s — it is difficult to be certain because earlier surveys did not ask appropriate questions relating to the topic — but suggest that this has nothing to do with dealignment. Rather, it reflects the fact that more seats are now contested by third and fourth parties, thus allowing more opportunities for people to vote tactically.[2] In the 1992 BES cross-section survey, however, the proportion of avowedly tactical voters rose to 8.7 per cent — certainly the largest it has been on Heath *et al.*'s definition — without any significant change in the pattern of party competition.

This is reflected in the election results. Although tactical voting can and does involve switching between all competing parties, Curtice and Steed (1992) concentrate on switching between Labour and the Liberal Democrats and show that in the 1992 election the swing from Conservative to Labour, and the decrease in the Liberal Democrat share of the vote, was greater in Conservative–Labour marginals than elsewhere. Moreover, the greater the size of the 1987 Alliance vote, the greater was the swing. And, at least in some areas, where the Alliance had been clearly in second place, the Liberal Democrat performance was better than average and Labour's worse. Curtice and Steed conclude that tactical voting may have cost the Conservatives ten seats.

The electoral system

I noted in Chapter 6 that one of the consequences of long-term geographical trends in party support has been to reduce the exag-gerative quality of the electoral system and that in 1992 the elec-toral system failed to give any bonus in seats to the winning party in terms of votes. But there is more to it than that. In 1992 the electoral system clearly benefited Labour and John Curtice (1992) calls this the 'hidden surprise' of the election. Labour should have expected a gain of twenty seats on the basis of the overall swing but in fact gained forty. This was for three reasons. First, Labour did better in marginal than in safe or hopeless seats; second, Labour-held constituencies have smaller electorates than non-Labour seats; third, turn-out in Labour seats was lower than in other seats. As a consequence, Labour won more seats than their overall share of the vote would have entitled them to under normal circumstances. If the next election were fought on the same con-stituency boundaries and there was a uniform swing, then a 0.5 per cent Conservative to Labour swing would rob the Conservatives of their overall majority, and Labour would become the largest party in the House of Commons if they achieved a 2.3 per cent swing, even though this would still leave them three points behind the Conservatives in terms of votes cast.

Table 7.3 Party choice of selected social sub-groups, 1992.

	Con.	Lab.	Lib. Dem.
Men aged 18–24	39	35	18
Women aged 18–24	30	43	19
Men aged 25–34	40	37	17
Women aged 25–34	40	38	18
Men aged 34–54	40	37	19
Women aged 34–54	46	32	19
Men aged 65+	44	38	16
Women aged 60+	51	31	17
Non-manual men	53	23	21
Non-manual women	55	22	20
Skilled manual men	37	43	16
Skilled manual women	40	38	18
Unskilled manual men	27	53	15
Unskilled manual women	33	47	15
Unemployed men	24	52	17
Unemployed women	26	51	16
Manual owner-occupiers	41	39	17
Manual council tenants	22	58	15
Non-manual private sector	61	19	19
Non-manual public sector	45	30	22
Manual private sector	31	50	18
Manual public sector	35	47	16

Note: The rows do not sum to 100 because votes for other parties are not shown.

Sources: Data relating to sector of employment are from Sanders (1992, p. 189); all other data are from MORI, reported in *The Times*, 11 April 1992.

Social groups and party choice

In Chapter 3 I discussed recent trends in the party choice of different groups within the electorate. Table 7.3 gives more detail for the 1992 election by showing how different sub-groups (i.e. people identified by two characteristics rather than one) voted.

The table makes clear Labour's relative strength among younger women. Whether these voters were attracted to Labour because of its more caring image or because it is more clearly identified with feminist concerns is difficult to say. Whatever it is, however, it clearly failed to attract older women — among those aged over 34 the gender gap is clear. The political differences between men and women also appear to be concentrated in the working class — women from manual households were significantly more likely to have voted Conservative rather than Labour as compared with male manual workers. Among unemployed people, however, Labour had a large lead among both sexes. The way in which housing tenure and sector of employment dampens class voting is also evident. Manual workers who are owner-occupiers gave a plurality of votes to the Conservatives while most middle-class public sector workers did not vote Conservative.

Another feature of the data in Table 7.3 is the relative evenness of Alliance support across different groups. This ranged only from 15 per cent among the unskilled and council tenants to 22 per cent in the public-sector middle class — a much narrower range than is the case with the other parties. The Liberal Democrats did have special appeal to one segment of the population, however — those who have had a university education. Among the (very small) group of graduates the Liberal Democrats won 30 per cent of the vote (compared with 39 per cent Conservative and 27 per cent Labour).[3]

Although I have argued that social characteristics have been a declining influence upon party choice in Britain, Table 7.3 is a useful reminder that they still have a part to play. Different social groups still tend to support different parties. For this reason, long-term changes in the social structure — some groups are increasing in size while others are declining — continues to have important implications for the fortunes of the parties. Richard Rose (1992) argues that, from a long-term perspective, there was nothing surprising about the Conservative victory in 1992. The social groups from which Labour can expect substantial support have been declining in size and this has eroded the vote that Labour can expect to achieve in 'normal' circumstances. On this basis, Rose suggests that the chances of Labour gaining an overall majority at the next election are very slim.

Judgemental voting

No comprehensive account has been published as yet of the extent to which party choice in the 1992 election was determined by voters' opinions, preferences and attitudes relating to policies, issues, performance and leaders — by what, in Chapter 4, I described as 'judgemental voting'. Plenty of relevant data are available, however, and these appear to present commentators with something of a puzzle. On what appear to have been the most important issues in the election Labour, and not the Conservatives, seems to have been the most favoured party. Crewe (1992b) suggests that the campaign agenda was less favourable to Labour than it first appears, since Labour's lead on issues like unemployment and health was actually smaller than in 1987. None the less, if the voters had followed their preferences on the issues that they said were important, Labour would have won, and on this basis Sanders (1992, pp. 194–7) argues that 'issue voting' was not significant.

As I have suggested, however, this is a narrow definition of issue voting, taking no account of other judgements that the electorate may have made — about the party leaders (where the Conservatives had a large lead), about the relationship between their own general ideological stances or principles and those of the parties (about which no evidence is available) or about the past and future performance of the economy.

The last example raises the question of economic voting. Kenneth Newton (1993) suggests that, on the face of it, the 1992 election presents a challenge to the theory of economic voting. Manifestly the economy was in poor shape and the voters were well aware of this. On past experience they should have voted the government out. One essential ingredient of economic voting was missing, however — the voters did not blame the government. Most blamed either the world-wide recession or Mrs Thatcher; hardly anyone blamed Mr Major's government as he had been in office for less than eighteen months. By removing Mrs Thatcher in November 1990 the Conservatives not only ditched an unpopular Prime Minister but also, indirectly, escaped being held responsible for the weakness of the economy. Indeed, Sanders argues that the Conservative victory can be explained almost entirely in economic terms. He concludes that Conservatives won because they convinced enough voters that 'the modest recovery in their personal economic circumstances that they had recently experienced was more likely to be sustained under a Conservative government than a Labour one' (1992, p. 183). Even if narrowly defined issue voting does not explain the result of the 1992 election very effectively, therefore, it is clear that voters' wider judgements were crucial.

The electoral outlook

Predicting future electoral trends — unlike 'predicting' from regression equations — is a hazardous business. It is particularly hazardous in Britain today because of the change from aligned to dealigned voting, which I have emphasised throughout this book. A commentator on elections writing in, say, 1955, could have felt confident in assuming that in the next few elections the two major parties would continue to dominate and that in terms of popular support they would not be very far apart. The electoral turmoil of the 1970s was still some way distant. With a dealigned, more free-floating electorate, however, the electoral situation is altogether more complex. None the less, I will conclude this review of electoral behaviour in Britain by considering briefly how the developments that have been discussed have affected the major parties, and by speculating a little about what the future might hold for them.

Table 7.4 provides further evidence relating to partisan dealignment, showing how each of the major parties has been affected, and I shall refer to this table as I discuss each of the major parties in turn.

Table 7.4   Identification with the major parties, 1964–92 (%).

	1964	1966	1970	Feb. 1974	Oct. 1974	1979	1983	1987	1992
Conservative % identifiers	39	35	39	35	34	38	36	37	45
'very strong'	48	49	51	32	27	24	25	23	21
Labour % identifiers	42	45	42	40	40	36	31	30	33
'very strong'	51	50	47	41	36	29	28	26	24
Liberal etc. % identifiers	11	10	8	13	14	11	17	16	13
'very strong'	32	35	26	12	14	14	21	10	8

Sources: Sarlvik and Crewe (1983, pp. 334–7); 1983, 1987 and 1992 BES cross-section surveys.

The Conservatives

Following the 1992 election the Conservative party appeared to be in a strong position. In not very auspicious circumstances they had won their fourth successive election and in each of them their share of the vote was very stable. Three factors point to their enjoying continuing electoral success in future.

First, long-term social changes — the contraction of the traditional working class, the increase in home ownership, the widening of share ownership, the movement of population from the North to the South, and so on — have worked to their advantage and will continue to do so. The social groups that have favoured the Conservatives are increasing in size and, to the extent that different groups support different parties, this gives them a long-term advantage. Second, in the last three elections the opposition to the Conservatives has been seriously divided. The split in the Labour party which led to the formation of the SDP in 1981 meant that Labour's position as the sole credible alternative to the Conservatives was significantly undermined. Anti-Conservative voters were no longer concentrated in one party. In Scotland and Wales non-Conservatives are even more fragmented. This fragmentation of opposition means that, even though the Conservative share of the votes has been small as compared with the 1950s and 1960s, their position seems relatively secure. Third, as the governing party, the Conservatives are in a position to influence the economic cycle such that, as far as possible, 'good times' return in the run-up to the next election (and elections after that). These sorts of considerations have led some commentators to conclude that Britain now has a 'dominant' (rather than 'competitive') party system in which the Conservatives can normally expect to win elections (see Crewe, Norris and Waller, 1992).

But some caution needs to be exercised before concluding that Conservative electoral hegemony will last for as far as anyone can foresee. In the first place, the extent of Conservative dominance in the last four elections should not be exaggerated. In each their share of the vote was smaller than it was in 1964 (when they lost) and markedly lower than they achieved in elections during the 1950s. The Conservative majorities in the House of Commons in the last four elections have been products of a divided opposition and (until 1992) the operation of the electoral system, rather than of great popularity among the voters. Second, although she eventually became very unpopular, there is no doubt that during the 1980s Mrs Thatcher was, overall, a significant electoral asset for the Conservatives. Mr Major was still enjoying a 'honeymoon' with the voters at the 1992 election but has since become less popular. It could be the case that in future elections the leadership factor will bring less of an electoral bonus to the Conservatives than it has since 1983. Third, the effect of a strengthened centre party is double-edged. Although it divides opposition, it also makes defecting easier. This is clear from by-election results. Many Conservative voters who would never dream of switching to Labour are willing to vote Liberal Democrat. In the 1992 general election, fear of 'letting Labour in' reduced defections to the centre, but the extra option remains and weak Conservatives could be tempted by the Liberal Democrats if they were unhappy with some aspects of government performance or policy.

Finally, the Conservatives, like the other parties, have suffered from the process of partisan dealignment. Identification with the Conservatives has held up relatively well over almost thirty years and in 1992 was higher than ever (see Table 7.4). But among these identifiers there has been a marked decline in the strength of their commitment to the party. By 1992, only about a fifth of Conservative identifiers were 'very strong' supporters of the party as compared with about half up to 1970. The Conservatives have been relatively successful in garnering votes at the last four elections but their supporters' commitment to the party is less than wholehearted. The identification data suggest that it is wrong to regard the stable forty-odd per cent of the vote gained by the Conservatives in the last few elections as representing a solid core vote. The real core — very strong identifiers — is much smaller.

Given this, it is always possible that if short-term factors, especially, perhaps, the voters' assessments of government performance on the economy, begin to go against them, then votes could flow away from the Conservatives just as quickly as they flooded to them in 1979. Governing a modern industrial society is complex and difficult and all governments run into problems. Moreover, the modern electorate is better informed and perhaps more critical than ever. Judgemental voting can be volatile and unstable, and a run of bad economic luck at the wrong time might put the Conservatives in an awkward position electorally. It would be wrong to assume, then, that social change, a weak opposition and past success in government assure the Conservatives of continued electoral success in future.

Labour

It must be said, however, that the outlook for the Conservatives looks decidedly rosy when compared with the position in which the Labour party now finds itself. The 1983 election had been an unmitigated disaster for the party, but at least part of the blame for that could be ascribed to short-term problems — divisions within the party leading to the formation of the SDP, an unpopular leader, a chaotic campaign organisation and an election manifesto that attracted much derision ('the longest suicide note in history', according to one senior Labour figure). In addition, the Falklands war, presided over by Mrs Thatcher, was still fresh in the minds of the electorate. Labour recovered only modestly in 1987 but could still take comfort from safely holding on to second place and beginning to make the party 'electable' again.

In 1992, however, Labour's long-term electoral problems were clearly highlighted. The economy was in deep recession, the poll tax had been wildly unpopular and government policies on health and education were widely criticised. Labour had made great efforts to modernise its image and make its policies more appealing to the voters, and was thought by all observers to have run the most professional and well-organised campaign. Yet Labour lost again. Moreover, in terms of the distribution of the votes, Labour's defeat was severe.

The causes of Labour's electoral problems are complex but three basic difficulties stand out. First, in stark contrast to the Conservatives, social changes have worked against Labour. The social groups among whom Labour's appeal is strongest — manual workers, council tenants, workers in heavy industry, people who live in the North — are declining segments of the electorate. To have a chance of winning power, Labour has to broaden its appeal and attract more support among the 'new' working class, home-owners, people living in the South and Midlands, and so on, as well as 'deepening' its support among traditional areas of strength. The importance of broadening the geographical base is emphasised by the fact that when constituency boundaries are redrawn (as they probably will be before the next election), there will inevitably be more constituencies in the South and fewer in the North (to take account of changes in population).

Second, partisan dealignment has had a particularly bad effect on Labour, as Table 7.4 shows. In contrast to the Conservatives, the proportion of the electorate identifying with Labour has clearly declined since the 1960s. At the 1979 election Labour (36 per cent) fell narrowly behind the Conservatives (38 per cent) for the first time in terms of this indicator of the level of basic support, but the gap has widened since then and in 1992 stood at 12 points. In addition, even among the declining numbers of Labour identifiers, the proportion very strongly committed to the party has halved.

In the past, many people regularly voted Labour out of class and party loyalty even when they were lukewarm about, if not hostile to, Labour policies. As this kind of aligned voting has become less common, Labour's policies and performance have become more relevant to the voters' decisions and, on the whole, they do not appear to have been very impressed. In particular in 1992, it appears that the voters had doubts about Labour's ability to run the economy and also disapproved of Labour's plans to increase taxation. Since it is unlikely that class and party loyalty will return to the levels of the 1950s and 1960s, it would appear that Labour's only realistic option is to make its policies more attractive to the electorate and somehow to convince voters that it can manage the economy more effectively than the government. Otherwise Labour can simply hope that something will turn up, that the government will make mistakes and thus allow Labour to win by default.

The third problem is, however, that Labour's complicated party structure and decision-making processes — based on a commitment to a form of intra-party democracy which has to take account of affiliated trade unions as well as local constituency parties — make it difficult to change party policies. Labour leaders appear to spend a lot of their time coping with the internal politics of the party, rather than working out what should be done about Labour's long-term electoral decline. Proposals for policy changes provoke furious internal debate and, if long-cherished policies are abandoned, this could alienate the most committed party members. As noted in Chapter 3, there is a strong body of opinion among Labour party members that would prefer the party to stick to its principles rather than change policies in order to win elections.

On the other hand, there are some positive things that can be said about Labour's prospects. One of the party's electoral problems in recent years has been the persistent unpopularity of the party leader — first Michael Foot and then Neil Kinnock. Mr Kinnock resigned almost immediately after the 1992 election and was replaced by John Smith. It may be that Mr Smith will prove to have greater electoral appeal than the last two leaders, although this must remain uncertain for the moment. What is clear, however, is that the Labour leadership has recognised that there have been problems associated with the party's structure and policies and realises that something has to be done. Comprehensive policy reviews have been undertaken; important changes in the party's rules, relating to such matters as the voting power of trade unions at the party conference and the direct participation of all members in internal party elections, have been made; people associated with far-left groups have been expelled from the party. It seems likely, too, that Labour's campaigning is at least the equal of that of the Conservatives.

The fact that Labour continues to be very strong in Scotland, Wales and the North of England has important consequences. It means that even if Labour's share of the national vote declines, they will still win a substantial number of seats in the House of Commons. In 1983, Labour was only narrowly ahead of the Alliance in terms of popular support, but won more than ten times as many seats. Labour consequently enjoyed the status of official Opposition and this brings many privileges in the conduct of business in the House, as well as extensive media coverage.

There are two main interpretations of Labour's performance in the 1992 election and of its future prospects (see Rose, 1992; Crewe, Norris and Waller, 1992). On the one hand, it can be argued that Labour increased its share of the vote, reversed its decline in the South, took many more second places than in 1987 and nearly won enough seats to deny the Conservatives an overall majority. On this view, what is needed to win the next election is 'one more heave' and the swing required to dislodge the Conservatives is very small. The second interpretation suggests that, given all the short-term circumstances in their favour, Labour should have done better. The closeness of the result in terms of seats is deceptive, since the electoral system, unusually, gave the second party in terms of votes a 'bonus' of seats. Given the problems referred to above, and the fact that circumstances are unlikely to be so favourable at the next election, the outlook for Labour is bleak.

One of the main arguments of this book has been that the electorate is now volatile and in that case nothing can be ruled out. Given a very favourable combination of short-term forces, it is not impossible that Labour could win power, or at least deny the Conservatives an overall majority. But, as far the next election is concerned, this remains an uphill task.

Liberal Democrats

In the two elections of 1983 and 1987, the SDP and the Liberals signally failed to 'break the mould' of British politics, although it might be said that they cracked it. The major hurdle that they faced, and failed to surmount, was the electoral system. The single-member, simple plurality system (or, more colloquially, 'first past the post') rewards parties whose support is concentrated and penalises those whose support is evenly spread. A third party could get a respectable level of support in every constituency — say, 30 per cent of the vote — and yet fail to win a single seat. Liberal Democrat support in 1992, like that for the Liberals before 1983 and for the Alliance in 1983 and 1987, was relatively similar among different social groups and, partly as a consequence of that, relatively even geographically. Across the ten regions shown in Table 7.2 the standard deviation of the Liberal Democrat share of the vote was 5.5, compared with 9.2 and 10.4 for the Conservatives and Labour respectively. This evenly spread support — despite some concentration in the South West — made it difficult for the Liberal Democrats to convert voting support into seats and explains why almost 18 per cent of the vote won them only 3 per cent of seats. The electoral system remains a major stumbling block for the Liberal Democrats.

A second feature of Liberal Democrat support which makes their position precarious is that they lack a substantial core of support that can be relied upon. As Table 7.4 shows, basic identification with the Liberal Democrats remains at a low level and only a very small proportion of their identifiers describe themselves as having a 'very strong' commitment to the Alliance — very much smaller, at 8 per cent of identifiers, than in the cases of the other parties.

A corollary of this is that the parties of the centre have tended to have unusually high 'recruitment' and low 'retention' rates at elections. That is, the percentage of voters for the party at one election who did not vote for it at the previous election is high, while the percentage of its voters at one election who continue to support it in the next election is low. Thus 51 per cent of people who voted Alliance in 1987 also voted Liberal Democrat in 1992 (retention rate) as compared with 79 per cent for the Conservatives and 78 per cent for Labour. On the other hand, 40 per cent of 1992 Liberal Democrat voters had *not* voted Alliance in 1987 (recruitment rate) compared with 22 per cent and 34 per cent for the Conservatives and Labour respectively.[4] A result of all these comings and goings is that centre-party voters do not appear to share any distinctive set of policy positions or even a vague, general ideology. Rather, the centre is viewed as a vehicle for expressing disaffection from other parties and is reliant on the major parties becoming unpopular and not on its own positive appeal. The Liberal Democrats appear to have inherited all of these problems.

From one perspective, however, the 1992 election could be said to have been a successful one for Mr Ashdown and his party. Immediately following the 1987 election the question of a merger between the Alliance partners — the Liberals and the SDP — was brought to the forefront of discussion. After much acrimonious debate, both parties voted to form a united party. Opponents of merger in the SDP, led by David Owen, refused to join the new party, however, and kept a separate SDP in existence. Many Liberals were also hesitant about joining the new party. The strains and divisions associated with the merger of the parties did not impress the voters. From 1988 to early 1991 opinion polls reported that support for the Liberal Democrats was as low as it had ever been in the whole post-war period. In the European Parliament elections held in June 1989 the Liberal Democrats were humiliated, winning just 6.4 per cent of the votes, less than half that obtained by the Green party (see Denver, 1992).

The general election result could be interpreted, therefore, as a major come-back from the low point in 1989 when the very existence of the party seemed to be threatened. The continuing SDP has disappeared and the Liberal Democrats are now the sole credible standard-bearers of the centre. Given that the electorate will remain dealigned, unstable and volatile, it is always possible that a combination of circumstances — the government becoming very unpopular, Labour failing to impress the voters as an alternative government — and a measure of good luck with regard to the timing of elections, might result in the election of enough Liberal Democrat MPs to deny any of the other parties a majority.

Conclusion

All of this is, of course, highly speculative. What is certain is that British electoral politics will continue to be more open and exciting than they were in the days of aligned voting. Dealignment and the increased importance of judgemental voting have created a situation in which the fortunes of the parties can alter very rapidly. Even the impression of stability given by four consecutive Conservative victories is misleading. The potential for rapid electoral change is greater than ever and for that reason among others, studying elections in the 1990s will continue to be fascinating — as well as good fun.

Notes

1. See *ICM Poll Review*, No. 9 (July 1992–January 1993).
2. It is worth pointing out, however, that the increase in third- and fourth-party candidates may itself be a consequence of dealignment, since they now have more chance of success than they did under a rigid two-party system.
3. These are Gallup data reported by Anthony King in the *Daily Telegraph*, 14 April 1992.
4. These figures are calculated from the BES 1987–92 panel and refer to respondents who were eligible to vote in both elections.

BIBLIOGRAPHY

Anwar, M. (1986), *Race and Politics*, Tavistock Publications.

Atkinson, M. (1984), *Our Masters' Voices*, Methuen.

Beer, S. (1982), *Britain Against Itself*, Faber.

Benney, M., A.P. Gray and R.H. Pear (1956), *How People Vote*, Routledge & Kegan Paul.

Berelson, B., P. Lazarsfeld and W. McPhee (1954), *Voting*, University of Chicago Press.

Blumler, J.G. and D. McQuail (1967), *Television in Politics*, Faber & Faber.

Bochel, J.M. and D. Denver (1970), 'Religion and voting: A critical review and a new analysis', *Political Studies*, vol. 18, no. 2, pp. 205–19.

Bochel, J.M. and D. Denver (1971), 'Canvassing, turnout and party support: An experiment', *British Journal of Political Science*, vol. 1, no. 3, pp. 257–69.

Brown, A. (1992), 'The Major effect: Changes in party leadership and government popularity', *Parliamentary Affairs*, vol. 45, no. 4, pp. 545–64.

Butler, D.E. and D. Kavanagh (1980), *The British General Election of 1979*, Macmillan.

Butler, D.E. and D. Kavanagh (1984), *The British General Election of 1983*, Macmillan.

Butler, D.E. and D. Kavanagh (1988), *The British General Election of 1987*, Macmillan.

Butler, D.E. and D. Kavanagh (1992), *The British General Election of 1992*, Macmillan.

Butler, D.E. and M. Pinto-Duschinsky (1971), *The British General Election of 1970*, Macmillan.

Butler, D.E. and D. Stokes (1969), *Political Change in Britain*, 1st edn, Macmillan.

Butler, D.E. and D. Stokes (1974), *Political Change in Britain*, 2nd edn, Macmillan.

Campbell, A., P. Converse, W. Miller and D. Stokes (1960), *The American Voter*, John Wiley.

Central Statistical Office (1993), *Social Trends*, HMSO.

Crewe, I. (1981a), 'Why the Conservatives won', in H. Penniman (ed.), *Britain at the Polls 1979*, American Enterprise Institute, Washington.

Crewe, I. (1981b), 'Electoral participation', in D. Butler, H.R. Penniman and A. Ranney (eds), *Democracy at the Polls*, American Enterprise Institute, Washington.

Crewe, I. (1984), 'The electorate: Partisan dealignment ten years on', in H. Berrington (ed.), *Change in British Politics*, Frank Cass.

Crewe, I. (1985a), 'Great Britain' in I. Crewe and D. Denver (eds), *Electoral Change in Western Democracies*, Croom Helm.

Crewe, I. (1985b), 'How to win a landslide without really trying', in A. Ranney (ed.), *Britain at the Polls 1983*, American Enterprise Institute, Washington.

Crewe, I. (1986), 'On the death and resurrection of class voting: Some comments on *How Britain Votes*', *Political Studies*, vol. 35, no. 4, pp. 620–38.

Crewe, I. (1988), 'Has the electorate become Thatcherite', in R. Skidelsky (ed.), *Thatcherism*, Basil Blackwell.

Crewe, I. (1992a), 'The 1987 general election', in Denver and Hands (eds), (1992).

Crewe, I. (1992b), 'Why did Labour lose (yet again)', *Politics Review*, vol. 2, no. 1, pp. 2–11.

Crewe, I. (1992c), 'Changing votes and unchanging voters', *Electoral Studies*, vol. 11, no. 4, pp. 335–45.

Crewe, I. (1992d), 'A nation of liars? Opinion polls and the 1992 election', *Parliamentary Affairs*, vol. 45, no. 4, pp. 475–95.

Crewe, I., N. Day and A. Fox (1991), *The British Electorate 1963–87*, Cambridge University Press.

Crewe, I., T. Fox and J. Alt (1977), 'Non-voting in British general elections 1966–October 1974', in C. Crouch (ed.), *British Political Sociology Yearbook*, vol. 3, Croom Helm.

Crewe, I., P. Norris, D. Denver and D. Broughton (eds), (1991), *British Elections and Parties Yearbook 1991*, Harvester Wheatsheaf.

Crewe, I., P. Norris and R. Waller (1992), 'The 1992 general election', in Norris, Crewe, Denver and Broughton (eds), (1992).

Crewe, I. and C. Payne (1971), 'Analysing the census data', in Butler and Pinto-Duschinsky (1971).

Crewe, I., B. Sarlvik and J. Alt (1977), 'Partisan dealignment in Britain 1964–1974', *British Journal of Political Science*, vol. 7, no. 2, pp. 129–90.

Curtice, J. (1992), 'The hidden surprise: The British electoral system in 1992', *Parliamentary Affairs*, vol. 45, no. 4, pp. 466–74.

Curtice, J. and M. Steed (1980), 'An analysis of the voting', in Butler and Kavanagh (1980).

Curtice, J. and M. Steed (1982), 'Electoral choice and the production of governments: The changing operation of the electoral system in the UK since 1955', *British Journal of Political Science*, vol. 12, no. 3, pp. 249–98.

Curtice, J. and M. Steed (1984), 'Analysis of the results', in Butler and Kavanagh (1984).

Curtice, J. and M. Steed (1986), 'Proportionality and exaggeration in the British electoral system', *Electoral Studies*, vol. 5, no. 3, pp. 209–28.

Curtice, J. and M. Steed (1988), 'Analysis', in Butler and Kavanagh (1988).

Curtice, J. and M. Steed (1992), 'The results analysed', in Butler and Kavanagh (1992).

Denver, D. (1992), 'The centre', in King (ed.), (1992).

Denver, D. and K. Halfacree (1992a), 'Inter-constituency migration and turnout at the British general election of 1983', *British Journal of Political Science*, vol. 22, no. 2, pp. 248–54.

Denver, D. and K. Halfacree (1992b), 'Inter-constituency migration and party support in Britain', *Political Studies*, vol. XL, no. 3, pp. 571–80.

Denver, D. and G. Hands (1974), 'Marginality and turnout in British general elections', *British Journal of Political Science*, vol. 4, no. 1, pp. 17–35.

Denver, D. and G. Hands (1985), 'Marginality and turnout in British general elections in the 1970s', *British Journal of Political Science*, vol. 15, no. 4, pp. 381–8.

Denver, D. and G. Hands (1990), 'Issues, principles or ideology? How young voters decide', *Electoral Studies*, vol. 9, no. 1, pp. 19–36.

Denver, D. and G. Hands (eds), (1992), *Issues and Controversies in British Electoral Behaviour*, Harvester Wheatsheaf.

Denver, D. and G. Hands (1993), 'Measuring the intensity and effectiveness of constituency campaigning in the 1992 general election', in Denver, Norris, Broughton and Rallings (eds), (1993).

Denver, D., P. Norris, D. Broughton and C. Rallings (eds), (1993), *British Elections and Parties Yearbook 1993*, Harvester Wheatsheaf.

Downs, A. (1957), *An Economic Theory of Democracy*, Harper: New York.

Dunleavy, P. (1980), 'The political implications of sectoral cleavages and the growth of state employment', *Political Studies*, vol. 28, nos. 3 and 4, pp. 364–83 and 527–49.

Dunleavy, P. (1987), 'Class dealignment in Britain revisited', *West European Politics*, vol. 10, no. 3, pp. 400–19.

Dunleavy, P. and C.T. Husbands (1985), *British Democracy at the Crossroads*, Allen & Unwin.

Eagles, M. and S. Erfle (1989), 'Community cohesion and voter turnout', *British Journal of Political Science*, vol. 19, no. 1, pp. 115–25.

Fallon, I. and R. Worcester (1992), 'The use of panel studies in British general elections', paper presented at EPOP/Political Communications conference, University of Essex, September 1992.

Franklin, M. (1985), *The Decline of Class Voting in Britain*, Oxford University Press.

Galbraith, J.W. and N.C. Rae (1989), 'A test of the importance of tactical voting: Great Britain 1987', *British Journal of Political Science*, vol. 19, no. 1, pp. 126–36.

Gallup (1992), *Gallup Political and Economic Index*, no. 380, July.

Glasgow University Media Group (1976), *Bad News*, Routledge & Kegan Paul.

Glasgow University Media Group (1980), *More Bad News*, Routledge & Kegan Paul.

Glasgow University Media Group (1982), *Really Bad News*, Writers and Authors Co-operative: London.

Goldthorpe, J.H., D. Lockwood, F. Bechhofer and J. Platt (1968), *The Affluent Worker*, 3 vols, Cambridge University Press.

Goodhart, C. and R. Bhansali (1970), 'Political economy', *Political Studies*, vol. XVIII, no. 1, pp. 43–106.

Harrison, M. (1985), *TV News: Whose Bias?*, Policy Journals, Hermitage: Berkshire.

Harrop, M. (1982), 'Labour-voting conservatives: Policy differences between the Labour party and Labour voters', in R. Worcester and M. Harrop (eds), *Political Communication: The General Election Campaign of 1979*, Allen & Unwin.

Harrop, M. (1986), 'Press coverage of post war British elections', in I. Crewe and M. Harrop (eds), *Political Communications: The General Election Campaign of 1983*, Cambridge University Press.

Harrop, M., A. Heath and S. Openshaw (1992), 'Does neighbourhood influence voting behaviour – and why?', in Crewe, Norris, Denver and Broughton (eds), (1991).

Heath, A., J. Curtice, R. Jowell, G. Evans, J. Field and S. Witherspoon (1991), *Understanding Political Change*, Pergamon.

Heath, A. and S. McDonald (1987), 'Social change and the future of the left', *Political Quarterly*, vol. 58, no. 4, pp. 364–77.

Heath, A. and R. Pierce (1992), 'It was party identification all along: Question order effects on reports of party identification in Britain', *Electoral Studies*, vol. 11, no. 2, pp. 93–105.

Heath, A., R. Jowell and J. Curtice (1985), *How Britain Votes*, Pergamon.

Heath, A., R. Jowell and J. Curtice (1987), 'Trendless fluctuation: A reply to Crewe', *Political Studies*, vol. 35, no. 2, pp. 256–77.

Hughes, C. and P. Wintour (1990), *Labour Rebuilt*, Fourth Estate.

Johnston, R. and C. Pattie (1991), 'Tactical voting in Great Britain in 1983 and 1987: An alternative approach', *British Journal of Political Science*, vol. 21, no. 1, pp. 95–128.

Johnston, R.J., C.J. Pattie and J.G. Allsop (1988), *A Nation Dividing*, Longman.

Kavanagh, D. (1971), 'The deferential English: A comparative critique', *Government and Opposition*, vol. 6, no. 3, pp. 333–60.

King, A. (1975), 'Overload: Problems of governing in the 1970s', *Political Studies*, vol. 23, nos. 2–3, pp. 284–96.

King, A. (ed.), (1992), *Britain at the Polls*, Chatham House: New Jersey.

Layton-Henry, Z. (1988), 'Black participation in the general election of 1987', *Talking Politics*, vol. 1, no.1, pp. 20–4.

Lazarsfeld, P., B. Berelson and H. Gaudet (1968), *The People's Choice*, 3rd edn, (1st edn 1944), Columbia University Press.

Lutz, J.M. (1991), 'Marginality, major third parties and turnout in England in the 1970s and 1980s: A reanalysis and extension', *Political Studies*, vol. XXXIX, no. 4, pp. 720–6.

McAllister, I. and R. Rose (1984), *The Nationwide Competition for Votes*, Frances Pinter.

McKenzie, R. and A. Silver (1968), *Angels in Marble*, Heinemann.

McLean, I. (1973), 'The problem of proportionate swing', *Political Studies*, vol. 21, no. 1, pp. 57–63.

McLean, I. (1982), *Dealing in Votes*, Martin Robertson.

McMahon, D., A. Heath, M. Harrop and J. Curtice (1992), 'The electoral consequences of North–South migration', *British Journal of Political Science*, vol. 22, no. 4, pp. 419–43.

Messina, A.M. (1989), *Race and Party Competition in Britain*, Clarendon Press.

Mill, J.S. (1963), *Considerations on Representative Government*, World Classics edn, Oxford University Press.

Miller, W.L. (1977), *Electoral Dynamics*, Macmillan.

Miller, W.L. (1978), 'Social class and party choice in England: A new analysis', *British Journal of Political Science*, vol. 8, no. 3, pp. 257–84.

Miller, W.L. (1979), 'Class, region and strata at the British general election of 1979', *Parliamentary Affairs*, vol. 32, no. 4, pp. 376–82.

Miller, W.L. (1991), *Media and Voters*, Clarendon Press.

Miller, W., H. Clarke, M. Harrop, L. Leduc and P. Whiteley (1990), *How Voters Change*, Clarendon Press.

Miller, W., S. Tagg and K. Britto (1986), 'Partisanship and party preference in government and opposition: The mid-term perspective', *Electoral Studies*, vol. 5, no. 1, pp. 31–46.

Milne, R.S. and H.C. MacKenzie (1958), *Marginal Seat*, Hansard Society: London.

Mughan, A. (1993), 'Party leaders and presidentialism in the 1992 election: A post-war perspective', in Denver, Norris, Broughton and Rallings (eds), (1993).

Newton, K. (1991), 'Do people read everything they believe in the papers? Newspapers and voters in the 1983 and 1987 elections', in Crewe, Norris, Denver and Broughton (eds), (1991).

Newton, K. (1993), 'Economic voting in the 1992 general election', in Denver, Norris, Broughton and Rallings (eds), (1993).

Nicholas, H.G. (1951), *The British General Election of 1950*, Macmillan.

Niemi, R., G. Whitten and M. Franklin (1992), 'Constituency characteristics, individual characteristics and tactical voting in the 1987 British general election', *British Journal of Political Science*, vol. 22, no. 2, pp. 229–54.

Nordlinger, E. (1967), *Working-Class Tories*, Macgibbon & Kee.

Norpoth, H. (1992), *Confidence Regained: Economics, Mrs Thatcher and the British Voter*, University of Michigan Press: Ann Arbor.

Norris, P. (1987), 'Four weeks of sound and fury . . . the 1987 British election campaign', *Parliamentary Affairs*, vol. 4, no. 4, pp. 458–67.

Norris, P. (1990), *British By-elections*, Clarendon Press.

Norris, P. (1993), 'The gender-generation gap in British elections', in Denver, Norris, Broughton and Rallings (eds), (1993).

Norris, P., I. Crewe, D. Denver and D. Broughton (eds), (1992), *British Elections and Parties Yearbook 1992*, Harvester Wheatsheaf.

Parkin, F. (1967), 'Working-class Conservatives: A theory of political deviance', *British Journal of Sociology*, vol. 18, no. 3, pp. 278–90.

Pattie, C., E. Fieldhouse, R. Johnston and A. Russell (1992), 'A widening regional cleavage in British voting behaviour, 1964–87: Preliminary explorations', in Norris, Crewe, Denver and Broughton (eds), (1991).

Pattie, C., R. Johnston and E. Fieldhouse (1993), 'Plus ça change? The changing electoral geography of Great Britain, 1979–92', in Denver, Norris, Broughton and Rallings (eds), (1993).

Pulzer, P.G. (1967), *Political Representation and Elections in Britain*, Allen & Unwin.

Rose, R. (1974), 'Britain: Simple abstractions and complex realities', in R. Rose (ed.), *Electoral Behaviour*, Free Press: New York.

Rose, R. (1980), 'Class does not equal party', Occasional Paper No. 74, Centre for the Study of Public Policy, University of Strathclyde.

Rose, R. (1985), 'Opinion polls as feedback mechanisms: From cavalry charge to electronic warfare', in A. Ranney (ed.), *Britain at the Polls 1983*, American Enterprise Institute, Washington.

Rose, R. (1992), 'Structural change or cyclical fluctuation? The 1992 election in dynamic perspective', *Parliamentary Affairs*, vol. 45, no. 4, pp. 451–65.

Rose, R. and I. McAllister (1986), *Voters Begin to Choose*, Sage: London.

Rose, R. and I. McAllister (1990), *The Loyalties of Voters*, Sage: London.

Runciman, W.G. (1966), *Relative Deprivation and Social Justice*, Routledge & Kegan Paul.

Sanders, D. (1991), 'Government popularity and the next general election', *Political Quarterly*, vol. LXII, pp. 235–61.

Sanders, D. (1992), 'Why the Conservatives won – again', in King (ed.), (1992).

Sanders, D. (1993), 'Forecasting the 1992 British general election outcome: The performance of an economic model', in Denver, Norris, Broughton and Rallings (eds), (1993).

Sanders, D., H. Ward and D. Marsh (1987), 'Government popularity and the Falklands war: A reassessment', *British Journal of Political Science*, vol. 17, no. 3, pp. 281–313.

Sarlvik, B. and I. Crewe (1983), *Decade of Dealignment*, Cambridge University Press.

Seyd, P. and P. Whiteley (1992), *Labour's Grass Roots*, Clarendon Press.

Startup, R. and E.T. Whittaker (1982), *Introducing Social Statistics*, Allen & Unwin.

Steed, M. (1966), 'An analysis of the results', in D.E. Butler and Anthony King, *The British General Election of 1966*, Macmillan, pp. 271–95.

Steed, M. (1986), 'The core–periphery dimension of British politics', *Political Geography Quarterly*, vol. 5, pp. 91–103.

Stokes, D. (1992), 'Valence politics', in D. Kavanagh (ed.), *Electoral Politics*, Clarendon Press.

Swaddle, K. and A. Heath (1989), 'Official and reported turnout in the British general election of 1987', *British Journal of Political Science*, vol. 19, no. 4, pp. 537–51.

Teer, F. and J.D. Spence (1973), *Political Opinion Polls*, Hutchinson.

Trenaman, J. and D. McQuail (1961), *Television and the Political Image*, Methuen.

Wallas, G. (1910), *Human Nature in Politics*, Constable.

Whiteley, P. (1986), 'The accuracy and influence of the polls in the 1983 general election', in I. Crewe and M. Harrop (eds), *Political Communications: The 1983 Election Campaign*, Cambridge University Press.

Whiteley, P. and P. Seyd (1992), 'Labour's vote and local activism: the impact of local constituency campaigns', *Parliamentary Affairs*, vol. 45, no. 4, pp. 582–95.

Worcester, R. (1992), 'How Labour swing fell short of the mark', *The Times*, 11 April.

INDEX